PRESENTED TO:

_____

FROM:

_____

DATE:

_____

NOW AVAILABLE!
OUR LSGA ONLINE SCHOOL!

If you like this book...

Then you will **LOVE** our 12 week online supernatural ministry school: the Love Says Go Academy.

More information www.LSGacademy.org

Join our next LSGA online school and **SAVE** on your school registration.

Get your **'Discount Code'** on pg. 247.

LOVESAYSGO

A *Supernatural Lifestyle*
Video Course

JASON CHIN

Acknowledgments

I have so many people to thank for helping me make this dream of mine a reality. I could not have done this without each and everyone of them. Each person mentioned volunteered their valuable time and energy to help me in this *Love Says Go* book & video project.

Thank you Aaron Mcmahon for being the first BSSM student to take the prophetic word of writing a book and doing it. That gave me the courage that I could write a book too. Sunneye Phillips, Joddi-Jay Babcock (my sister) and Richard Song, you helped edit my thoughts on paper into correct grammar and spelling. That was a huge feat and incredible blessing from God. Mike Skilleter, Matt Murnan, Liviu Zoe, Josiah and Jonah Dahlquist, your video equipment and media skills added excellence to this project.

Kristina Waggoner, Jason Tax, Alexander Logia, Jordan Dahlquist, Caleb Fiess, Richard Song, Mitch McCuen and other friends of Revival. Thank you for running through walls of fear and intimidation with me as we discovered the love of God for ourselves and others. Many of these stories you may remember since you were there.

Stephen Chin, Cambrea Chin and Brandon Chin (my children), you have inspired me as I see the greatness of God in each of you. You are some of my heroes!

Alan and Anne Chin (my parents), your lives of adoption has challenged me to love no matter the cost. I am so proud of who you are.

Joyce and Kent Berry (my parents). Mom, your life in Jesus has had one of the greatest impacts on my life. Kent, you are real funny.

I am so thankful for Bill Johnson and the Bethel Church family in Redding, California. The revival culture here has transformed my life.

Jesus I give You ALL the glory and honor of this *Love Says Go* video project. Heaven knows this was only possible in You. I pray that many lives will be eternally impacted by your love, presence and power. In Jesus name!

ENDORSEMENTS

Love Says Go is not just a book — it is a lifestyle. It is not a theory or a great idea — it is a practical manual for the Christian life. In John 3:16, God so loved the world that He sent His one and only Son; He said to His Son, "Go," and because of His love for us He went. In Matthew 28:19, Jesus told His disciples to, "Go." Jason Chin is one of the best models of "Going" that I can think of. *Love Says Go* will not only equip you to "Go," but will empower you to "Go." You will find practical activations that will enable you to "Go" to the world that God still loves.

This is not just another book about witnessing — it is a guide to doing what Jesus did. *Love Says Go* will not just tell you to "Go," but will motivate you to "Go." Jason will take you on a journey into encountering God's love, cultivating God's love, and releasing God's love in practical, powerful, supernatural ways to demonstrate His great love to those around you. If you want to be a world changer, buy it, read it, do it! You will never be the same, and the world around you will not be the same!

Kevin Dedmon
Pastor, Bethel Church - Redding, California
Author of: *The Ultimate Treasure Hunt,*
Unlocking Heaven and *The Risk Factor*

Jason is a revivalist in every sense of the word. He's climbed the waterfall of "fear of man;" he's swum the moat of doubt and unbelief; and is now storming the castle for souls and demonstrations of the Kingdom of Heaven. I love how he is bringing both literal step by step instruction on how to walk in miracles and an online demo pack allowing people to watch and learn from seeing the process walked out. This innovative approach to training is cutting edge and will lead many into the practice of the supernatural. I expect that this will be a model for many future authors and I am happy to endorse Jason Chin's first work of heart!

Danny Silk
Senior Leadership Team, Bethel Church – Redding, California
Author of *Culture of Honor*
Practice of Honor and *Powerful & Free*

Jason is someone I admire not only for what is written in this powerful message, but for all that can't be shared in mere words. *Love Says Go* is much more than a book, it's a map of love that we can actually see come alive and step into with all our hearts! It will lead you on a fresh journey with Jesus that has unending possibilities, and it is packed with a love so rich you will find courage you never knew you had to live out your true identity in Christ.

Jason has creatively developed this book to walk alongside you, and teaches what it means to reveal the nature of the Father to all people, wherever you go. Jason is as authentic as they come, and passionately in love with his God! You can witness such for yourself and be inspired to live the fullness God has uniquely created you to shine to the world. Many people have a passion to reach others with Jesus, but don't know where to begin. Start here. Start with love! And GO wherever He sends you!

Joey LeTourneau
Heavenly Hope Ministries - Denver, Colorado
Author of *Revolutionary Freedom* and *The Life Giver*

Jason is a friend and one of the most committed individuals I know that has chosen to overcome fear with love. I recommend this book to ignite and activate passion to see the love of God manifested through Power through your life.

Chris Overstreet
Pastor, Bethel Church - Redding California
Author of *A Practical Guide to Evangelism Supernaturally*

TABLE OF CONTENTS

Videos & Activations

ACCESS YOUR ONLINE TRAINING VIDEOS

- Log into www.lovesaysgobook.com.

- Click on the VIDEO tab on the top left of the screen.

This post is password protected. To view it please enter your password below.

Password: 316J1038a | Submit

Protected: Chapter Videos

June 7, 2013

- The video password is: 316j1038a

- You will see the wordpress log in screen.

(W)WORDPRESS

Username

Password

☐ Remember Me   Log In

Register | Lost your password?

- Click on *Register* and set up a secure log in account for the online chapter videos.

FOREWORD

Love Says Go is bound to have a great impact on everyone who reads it. It is filled with life from cover to cover. And like other books that I have great esteem for, this one encourages, gives insight, and provokes the reader to discover what might be possible in their lifetime.

This book is inspired by Jason's own journey in the supernatural. Like most of the people who come to us for our training, he came to Bethel School of Supernatural Ministry very fearful. Fear is a natural byproduct of a flawed identity in Christ. He was too afraid to go to his evangelism activation sessions. Courage and boldness were subjects on a page, not experiences or a lifestyle for him. Yet, as a result of his success in this journey, he is now a leader and teacher in the area of his greatest previous weakness. In his quest for more, he wonderfully experienced a sustained breakthrough.

Jason's key for evangelism has three major points: Loving God, loving yourself and loving others. He shows that evangelism starts in our personal relationship with God, and that living aware of His presence is the top priority. He also illustrates how knowing our identity and properly loving ourselves is key to stepping out and loving others. His personal stories give practical examples of power-filled evangelism that should give every reader increased hunger and courage. In doing so, Jason equips the reader with a practical tool kit for prophecy, words of knowledge, and healing.

He also shares the importance of walking in power and of taking power out into the world, and then gives very practical ways to make the supernatural a part of your everyday life. He effectively combats the hurdles of fear and inadequacy. He deals with these issues with biblical insights and personal testimonies that make available the keys to overcome.

It is a great honor to commend to you this wonderful book, and this wonderful man. We have been encouraged by Jason Chin's message and lifestyle. His life has had a great impact on the work that God is doing here in our city. And through this book, it is sure to spread to more and more places, through more and more transformed lives. I welcome you to the journey of a lifetime.

Bill Johnson
Senior Leader Bethel Church - Redding, California
Author of *When Heaven Invades Earth, Dreaming with God, The Power of a Transformed Mind* and *Hosting the Presence*

INTRODUCTION

I have come to a personal conviction that every believer, regardless of age, personality type or ethnicity, is called to bring heaven to earth. My life was radically inflamed when I discovered that I was designed to live a supernatural life just like Jesus, full of the miraculous power and love of God. With some basic training this supernatural lifestyle can become very normal and natural.

The *Love Says Go* supernatural video course is my endeavor to help you in this journey. Along with this book, you get coinciding training videos--at least one training video per chapter. I am very excited about these hands-on activation videos where you get to practice what you are learning. It is practical "teach and do" supernatural equipping.

This training is aimed at three specific targets: Loving God, loving yourself and loving others. Our first mission is God Himself. He is to be sought after, experienced and enjoyed in close fellowship. Practicing His presence and recognizing His voice are top priorities. Second, it is essential that we walk in our proper identity in Christ and learn to love ourselves. The Bible says that we can only love others to the degree that we love ourselves (Mark 12:31). As we receive the unconditional love of Father God and adopt who

He says we are, then we are free and empowered to love the people around us. The final section in this book is hands-on equipping to love others in power. We cover basic prophecy, healing the sick and marketplace ministry. In each chapter I retell incredible personal accounts of God's supernatural intervention. I share powerful miracles of physical healing and other supernatural phenomena. I hope these testimonies will thoroughly encourage you.

While this training is geared toward an audience starting in their supernatural Jesus journey, I believe the truths and activations will help advance even the most experienced.

Much of the material in this training kit comes from my instruction at Bill Johnson's Bethel School of Supernatural Ministry (BSSM) in Redding, California. Prior to my enrollment in BSSM in 2006, I had never recognized the various ways God speaks or practiced His presence. I had never prophesied or prayed for the sick. After some simple equipping, I have been blessed to have had profound life-changing encounters in the Holy Spirit's presence. I have also been privileged to personally witness hundreds of miracles of physical healing, deliverance and salvation because of the love of Jesus!

I currently have the incredible honor to help train and equip students for our Treasure Hunt activation at BSSM. I speak at supernatural conferences and schools around the globe. My mission is to help equip the Body of Christ to walk in her rightful identity and move in His love and power.

Please visit my personal website at www.lovesaysgo.com for more supernatural training and miracle videos.

Chapter One

Stepping Into Your Supernatural Destinty

"If you live cautiously, your friends will call you wise. You just won't move many mountains." – Bill Johnson

"Jason what are you doing?" The Holy Spirit was speaking to my heart. I was presently sitting in my four-door Saturn sedan, skipping my Thursday Treasure Hunt outreach because of fear. It was the fourth consecutive week I had purposely skipped out on my supernatural activation at Bethel School of Supernatural Ministry (BSSM). We had just recently finished our first six weeks of supernatural training in school and now it was time to do the stuff in public that we had learned in the classroom. I had given my outreach team an excuse of why I needed to take my own car and meet them at our designated location. However, instead of meeting my team, I found myself parked at Wal-Mart sitting in my car alone praying loudly in emergency tongues. I was interceding for my team. I was supposed to be with my team in the community, reaching out to others in the power and love of Jesus, but because of fear I was hiding from my personal supernatural destiny God had fashioned for me.

> *"Gideon was beating out wheat in the winepress, to hide..."* (Judges 6:11 ESV).

FLURRY OF FLASHBACKS

While interceding in my car, my thoughts drifted to some dramatic life-altering events that had freshly transpired in my life. I thought about my recent prodigal son conversion experience in a little country church one year prior. I reflected on how God, Jehovah-Sneaky, had tricked me. God had set me up, answering the petitions of my Holy Spirit-filled, praying momma.

I had been telling my family for years, "I don't want to be a Christian. Christianity is way too boring for me." I had been off the Christian path for about 14 years. I walked away from Jesus to chase after the world's allurement. I felt I had obtained all that the world had to offer, and I thought I was the happiest of men. I had money, lots of it. I had impressive automobiles, girls and a reputation of success in business. I had worked my way up the corporate ladder and was a general manager of a family-owned company, making a healthy six-figure income in my early thirties. I was also the spiritual black sheep of my family. I was the only one in my immediate family that wasn't radically following Jesus. I was radical alright, but it was misdirected towards the devil. I didn't outright worship the devil, but all my actions proved who my god really was.

I was so hardened to the Gospel that I would not let anyone play Christian music in my presence. Although I didn't have the fear of God active in my life, I was completely afraid to die. I had the revelation that if I were to die, I would surely go to hell. I would sometimes ponder that thought and it scared me. I remember praying each time I got on an airplane, "God, I know I am living in sin, but if this plane goes down, please give me thirty seconds to get right with you. Please don't let me die without a chance to get right with you." I knew I was heading to hell, but I wanted a last chance life insurance policy on my deathbed. I didn't want to live for God, but I was afraid to die without Him. I wonder how many people today are in this same place of heart?

I had broken my left ankle from an alcohol-related incident and was off work recovering from surgery. My mother and my little sister had come to visit me. This was quite the power packed duo.

Here is a quick glimpse into my mother's life. While I was growing up, my mother and her close friend Sandy had read a book called *Pigs in the Parlor*. This book was about deliverance, so they decided to start a deliverance ministry right in our garage! They apparently thought it would be a good idea to start looking for the most demonized people in our city and then to invite them over to our house on Friday night to be set free. Our garage became the research and development room for these ladies to grow in knowledge and understanding in spiritual exorcism. I remember curiously putting my ear to the closed garage door. I would hear loud unusual sounds, shrieks and all sorts of commotion coming from inside our garage. It sounded at times like a war zone. It was God destroying the works of the devil in man. These ladies were setting people free. People's lives were radically getting changed in our two-car garage. Many times Mother would share the wild war stories of what happened the night before. These stories were very exciting and supernatural in nature and proved God's authority over the devil. Yet at the same time these stories of the demonic scared me and to tell you the truth, so did my exorcist warrior momma.

Okay, now let me tell you a little bit about my little sister, Sarah. Sarah is a straight shooter. She isn't one to mince her words. So with Mother close by, Sarah was the first to lay into me. "Jason, when are you going to grow up and get your life right?" She continued to point out truths in my life that I was unable to see or agree with at the time. She pointed down the road of my life, trying to show me where all my not-so-brilliant life decisions were taking me. I was blinded to the truth. I thought I was doing pretty well. I felt I was a genuinely happy and successful person. Although in reality, I had been consuming a steady diet of anti-depressant drugs for over ten years, and I was addicted to pornography and painkillers to medicate and dull all my inner hidden pain. I tried convincing my family that it was no use telling me about Jesus anymore. I plainly did not have any desire to serve Him.

A Brilliant Idea

As my sister continued talking, an extraordinary idea popped into my head. To prove to them that God wasn't my cup of tea, I would go to church just once to get them off my back. I would tell them afterward, "See, I tried it…It didn't work for me…Now please lay off my life!" So I planned it all out, and I found a safe little country church to attend. I took my children and even had my drinking buddy, Puga, go with me. As the service was coming to a close, I remember the feelings of triumph swelling up inside of me. I was anticipating my jubilant victory celebration, rehearsing my speech in my head, telling my family, "See Christianity is just not for me." In that moment the pastor had the nerve to utter these words, "Before we close the service, I have a feeling there are some people here that need to get their lives right with Jesus." Great panic hit. A bomb of anxiety instantly exploded inside my chest.

I recall the impact those words had on me. Heart pounding with hands sweating, I instinctively grabbed with a death grip the bottom of my pew. Breathing heavily, I closed my eyes and told myself, "Self, you just stay calm and focus. If he calls people to the altar up front to receive Jesus, you are NOT going no matter what! You just hang on for a few more minutes and this will all be over soon enough." Opening my eyes slightly, I could see the front of my shirt pulsating with every pounding heartbeat.

I glanced over to where Puga was sitting to see how he was fairing in this assault. To my utter shock and great dismay, the seat where Puga was sitting was now empty. Puga had responded to the pastor's altar call and was now half way down the aisle. He was quickly walking towards the front of the church to meet Jesus. Puga had given in to the pressure of the Holy Spirit and to the homecoming call of his Father in heaven.

I said to myself, "I guess Puga's history. I will just have to replace him with another drinking friend." Closing my eyes, I refocused all my strength and willpower to remain in my seat and in my sin. I told myself, "Self, you're doing real good. Puga may be gone, but you're gonna make it. You just sit tight. Take some deep breaths and remain calm. You're going to be just fine."

The only problem was the great Holy Spirit and that country pastor would just not let up. The pastor said this, "I'm going to give it a few more minutes, because I really feel in my spirit that there are more people in here that need to come up to this altar right now and get right with Jesus. I feel God is saying there are some people here that have walked away from the Lord Jesus and today is your day to come home."

THE FATHER'S EMBRACE

I just couldn't take it any longer! The pressure on my heart was too great and overpowering. I gave in. I got up from my seat and stepped into the aisle toward the altar. As soon as I hit the aisle, an eruption of God's love went off within me. I started to sob uncontrollably. I was crying so violently that I had a hard time seeing my way to the front of the church. Even now it's hard to explain the whirlwind of emotions that were occurring within my soul. All the pain and anger that was in my heart was being changed into forgiveness and love. Just as the prodigal son story goes in Luke 15, my heavenly Father was embracing me as His long lost beloved son. I found a Hispanic brother at the front of the church that led me in a simple sinner's prayer as I wept in God's loving presence.

I was completely undone by the Father's forceful and unrelenting love towards me. In spite of my indifference, defiance and willful darkness that I had shown towards Him, this radical love of

God plundered my heart and took me captive. I was changed in an instant by His love for me. I immediately started telling everyone I knew that it was Jesus we were searching for the whole time and we didn't even know it. I can attest to you that I am the same person today that was at the altar that night. I have grown in my awareness and nearness of a supernatural God, but my heart was completely changed and inflamed in love for Jesus in that moment. The addictions and medications that held me captive for so long dropped off my life. I was a changed man. Thank you, Jesus!

"Jason, what are you doing?" The Holy Spirit's voice brought my thoughts back to reality. I was still at Wal-Mart sitting in my parked car.

Again, "Jason, what are you doing?" Not wanting to answer the Holy Spirit's question, I pretended that I could not hear Him. Starting to pray in tongues, I looked down at my watch concluding that I only had another thirty minutes to hide out until my outreach was officially over for this week.

A GLIMPSE INTO ANOTHER WORLD

My thoughts then drifted to another memory. I remembered the first time that I had visited Bethel Church upon my mother's recommendation. I recalled what it felt like when I stepped into the sanctuary during worship. There was tingling-like electricity in the air. I was in awe of feeling God's tangible presence hovering around me as I worshiped Jesus. The presence of God in that building amazed me. That night I heard testimonies of modern-day miracles of supernatural physical healing. This was foreign to me.

In the little country church that I came from, I never recalled praying for the sick. It was new for me to hear these miracle stories that were happening at Bethel. I heard stories of cancerous tumors instantly dissolving. One second a tumor was there and after a quick prayer the tumor could not be found. I heard testimonies of blind eyes seeing and deaf ears hearing. I also heard stories of crippled limbs being restored just like new. This group of people celebrated and cheered over these incredible miracles. It seemed like this group expected to see miracles happen.

I looked around at all these unusual people in this service wondering, "Where am I? I feel like I stepped onto another planet or something. Who are these people, and is this stuff really true?" All these miracles that they shared happened not by a well-known televangelist overseas, but by a bunch of very normal looking people of all age groups. Many of the miracles they shared happened on the streets of Redding, California, in the U. S. A. I just couldn't believe it! My head was spinning. Something happened deep inside of my heart that night. God impregnating me with a deep hunger and passion that was crying out, "God, there is obviously so much more of You than I knew of...and...I have to have this for myself!"

Chris Overstreet, the outreach pastor, got up next to preach and I saw a human being so on fire with God's power, passion and love. Overwhelmed, I sat there crying. I was mesmerized by the amount of God I saw inside a man. It was different than any human I had seen in my life. I told God in that moment, "I don't care what it takes, Jesus. I have to know you like this man does!" That night I got to see a glimpse into another world, a world that didn't seem to have all the same limits, rules, and regulations as the one I had lived in my whole life. I felt so alive after hearing these supernatural miracle stories of my Jesus. That night I asked myself this question, "Is this life of a supernatural Jesus possible in my life too?" I enrolled in BSSM a couple months later to find out.

MIGHTY MAN OF COURAGE

"Jason, what are you doing?" Pondering the Holy Spirit's question, I thought, "What am I doing? Why am I skipping class, hiding in my car again?" I was so frustrated at myself for chickening out four weeks in a row; yet at the same time, I felt so intimidated, stuck and paralyzed from fear.

"Jason, hello? What are you doing?"

Realizing the Holy Spirit had all of eternity to ask that same irritating question and chances were He wasn't about to let up any time soon, I responded.

"Alright, Holy Spirit, You win. I know that You know that I heard You the whole time. You already know this I'm sure, but I'm skipping outreach activation because I am too afraid. I just can't get myself to do this. I really want to heal the sick. I just don't think I have what it takes. Boy, do I want to be bold and courageous, but I'm realizing this supernatural lifestyle thing must not be for me. I guess I am just not cut out for it."

Like Gideon, I was telling God all the reasons that I wasn't qualified to do great exploits with Him. I was telling God that somebody, either myself or Him, had made a big mistake.

Gideon said, *"O my Lord, how can I save Israel? Indeed my clan is the weakest in Manasseh, and I am the least in my father's house"*

(Judges 6:15). Perhaps you have felt like this too. Maybe you also have a dream and a desire burning in your heart to do great accomplishments with God. However, when push comes to shove, when the rubber hits the road, you catch yourself skipping out on your supernatural destiny, hiding in your own personal winepress of fear and praying for others from a distance. Maybe like Gideon, you do not know who you are yet. Gideon said he was the least of the weakest. He told God that he was the most unqualified for the job, but God saw Gideon quite differently. Who did God see Gideon to be?

> *"And the Angel of the Lord appeared to him and said to him, The Lord is with you, you mighty man of [fearless] courage" (Judges 6:12 AMP). The NIV translation says, "you, mighty warrior."*

I am sure Gideon was thinking, "Um, excuse me mister angel, but I am afraid you must be mistaking little ole me for someone else. I guess you do not realize that I'm actually hiding in a winepress right now from the Midianites because of FEAR. I hate to say it, but you're barking up the wrong tree. You really must have the wrong guy. Good luck finding your hero, mister angel."

Look how the Lord responds. Then the Lord turned to him and said, *"Go in this might of yours, and you shall save Israel from the hand of the Midianites. Have I not sent you?"* (Judges 6:14). Absolutely ignoring all of Gideon's laundry list of seemingly very valid disqualifications, God told Gideon he was, in fact, the right guy and it was time for him to go public with his faith.

God will continuously point us toward our true identity as He did with Gideon. He keeps ignoring all of our excuses of why we can't do this or do that with Him. He is saying very clearly and emphatically to us, "Mighty son or daughter of fearless courage, it's time to go public with your faith. Have I not sent you?"

SHOWING UP

With the help of the Holy Spirit, I committed to stop cutting class. I began the habit of getting out of my winepress of fear each week. I started attending my Thursday outreaches. For me this was my first gigantic breakthrough into my supernatural destiny. My first big step was going out with my team on outreach.

On outreach days I would wake up and realize, "Oh snap, it's Thursday!" Immediately, I would start making declarations over my life to encourage me not to skip class that day. I would say things like, "Jason, you are a healing revivalist called to the nations. Demons tremble at the Holy Spirit in you. You are a fearless lover of people." Each Thursday as I strengthened myself in the Lord and chose to show up and go out, it got a little bit easier for me to go out the following week. The resistance seemed to lessen each time I went out.

At first, during outreach days I would stand in the distance and watch my team pray for others. I began to witness pain leave some bodies as my team prayed for people. Encouraged, I eventually mustered up even more faith. If a person closed their eyes as my team prayed for them, I would quietly step over and touch them on the shoulder with the tip of my finger. If they said they were healed or the pain lessened, I would write in my miracle journal, "I healed a back today" or "I healed a knee today." I figured it should count because my finger touched them too.

In time with practice I began to learn how to recognize God's voice and I started to give basic prophetic words of encouragement. I eventually started to pray for physical healing in the marketplace. I was slowly launching out, into the deeper waters of my supernatural destiny to love others.

Getting Into the Water

When attempting to do something that is new, people have differing approaches, and that is to be expected. It is like going to the lake on a hot summer day and watching how people choose to get into the cool water. Some will sprint towards the lake, running into the water up to their waist and then dive in, completely submerging themselves under the surface. They don't appear daunted in the slightest with the chilliness of the water. Others will slowly meander to the water's edge and put their big toe in first, wiggling it around to check the temperature difference. If the water is not too frigid for their big toe, they will carefully inch their way into the water to reduce the shock of it. Eventually in time, they will be out freely swimming with the others.

Some people are thrill seekers that jump off high rock cliffs or take a rope swing to fling into the lake. They enjoy the adrenaline rush. Getting into the waters of your supernatural destiny is very similar to this. Everyone's approach and journey will look different. Some will jump right in. Others, like me, may take smaller baby steps. It is not so important how you choose to enter the waters of your God-given supernatural destiny, as long as you get in and get fully wet.

Like Gideon, as I grew in my awareness of God being with me

and, more importantly, His love toward me and others, I was able to overcome and defeat many of those Midianites of fear trying to keep me on the shore. Over the last few years, partnering with the great Holy Spirit, I have had the wonderful privilege to witness many of those same incredible miracles that I heard about during my initial visit to Bethel Church when I asked God and myself this question. "Is a life of the miraculous possible in my own life, too?" Now I can say I have seen first-hand blind eyes seeing, the deaf hearing, crippled limbs being restored, wheelchairs emptied, demons coming out of people with shrieks, and people being set free and saved by the power and love of Jesus that came through the Holy Spirit in me. Wow!

So the answer is a resounding, "Yes!" A lifestyle in the supernatural is not only available to me, it is for all of us in Christ! It is the normal way of life and it is our destiny in Jesus. So let's all get off the boring shores of limitation and get into the living waters of the kingdom of heaven. Let's jump in and enjoy this life in Him.

TESTIMONY - NEW HIPS IN HOME DEPOT

One of the supernatural outreaches that we do at BSSM is called Treasure Hunting. It is where we ask the Holy Spirit for specific clues, such as location, a person's appearance and their prayer needs. We then write them down on a treasure map and go out to find those clues that lead us to God's treasure--the person matching the appearance clues. We get to bless this treasure through a physical healing or prophetic word of encouragement. We will talk more about this fun way of supernatural evangelism in Chapter 11.

It was a Thursday afternoon Treasure Hunt outreach in first year BSSM. I was with two female classmates and our treasure map had led us to Home Depot. We were looking for our other clues when we noticed a middle-aged man walking with a cane. By the way, if you see someone with a cane, wheel chair or a brace you have an automatic green light to go ask if you can pray for them. We approached the man and his wife. They were inspecting the carpet rolls when we walked up.

We introduced ourselves, let them know about the Treasure Hunt and asked, "Sir, we noticed that you have a cane. Why do you need it?" Gary, the man with the cane said, "I have two bad hips and I am scheduled for two hip replacements." We asked him, "Can we pray for your hips? We have seen Jesus do some awesome miracles." We weren't lying; it was a true statement. We had seen Jesus heal in some miracle videos we watched at school. We saw videos of A. A. Allen, Jack Coe, Kathryn Kuhlman.

Gary looked at his wife, Jill, shrugged his shoulders and said, "Sure, why not?" The girls stepped on each side of Gary and put their hands on his shoulders. I bent down on one knee and put my hands on his hips. We all said, "Holy Spirit, come."

Gary's legs started to tremble. He started to shake increasingly with more intensity. I looked up at the girls with a gleeful look, silently expressing, "Wow, this is good!" Then--wham-- Gary's limp body hit the ground so hard, it almost bounced. No one had caught him. We hadn't even thought to. No one had ever gone down on us before when we had prayed for them. I thought, "This is awesome! Just like Benny Hinn." We looked at each other in bewilderment. We had no idea what to do. Gary's body was shaking violently on the ground. It looked like he was having a full-blown grand mal seizure. We all stood there staring at his body shaking on the ground. We didn't want to disturb him, thinking it might interrupt what God was doing.

I thought, "What do we say if an employee comes by and sees Gary's body shaking on the ground?" Those thoughts were interrupted by a voice saying, "What am I doing down here? Why am I on the ground?" We helped Gary stand back up to his feet and we steadied him, because his body was still trembling under God's power. "How did I end up on the ground?" he asked.

"We don't really know for sure. All we said was 'Holy Spirit, come.' Then you started to shake and you fell on your back." Gary replied, "When you started to pray for me, everything went pitch black and then I saw Jesus. Jesus smiled, walked up to me and touched my shoulder. He told me not to worry and that everything was going to be okay."

We asked Gary if he could check his hips out to see how they felt. After all it was Jesus Himself that he saw touch him. Gary started moving his hips back and forth and side to side. He stated, "I can't feel any pain. Wow, my hips feel great!" Uninhibited by having no more pain in his hips, Gary began waltzing around the store without his cane and started shouting loudly at the top of his lungs, "Jesus healed me…Jesus healed me… Jesus healed me!"

I thought, "Oh, no! We are definitely going to get kicked out of this store soon." Fortunately, we did not. Before we left, we all celebrated and thanked Jesus for this great miracle. We hugged and said our goodbyes for it was time to meet up with the rest of our team. After sharing this remarkable Jesus encounter with our team, our second year BSSM leader asked us if we had the opportunity to ask them about receiving Jesus for their salvation. Our response was, "Um, no...We totally forgot to do that...Oops!"

We were all very new, inexperienced, and unsure how to do much of this supernatural ministry stuff, but because of God's great ability to be in charge and the great Holy Spirit, Gary and Jill came to the next Friday night service. They both came up front and gave their lives to Jesus! Gary told us that he had canceled his hip surgery, too. Come on, Jesus! God is really big and He is good at His job, even when we do not have an inkling of what we are doing. That is some good news of the unveiling of the kingdom of heaven.

 ## Action Step

- Watch Video #1 - Dreaming With God

- Journal your experience

Chapter Two

THE KINGDOM OF HEAVEN IS HERE

"The kingdom of God is within you." – Jesus Christ

Jesus, John the Baptist and the twelve disciples all proclaimed this message, "Repent, for the kingdom of heaven is at hand." This was the first time the world had ever heard this radical statement. So what were they declaring? Let's break it down and take a look.

Repent is the Greek word metanoia. It is a compound word that means "to think differently after" or "a change of mind and heart."

Kingdom is the Greek word basileia meaning "royalty, to rule, a realm or an area that a king reigns over."

Hand in Greek is eggizo meaning "to make near, approach, to come near."

It is a declaration that it is time to think and act differently now, because there is a different kingdom that has just arrived. Just as in Jesus' day, this kingdom, God's kingdom, is here now. It is very close and completely available to us. All the rules have changed, so we need to alter the way we think and embrace His kingdom, the kingdom of heaven.

THE VEIL IS TORN

As Christians everything that separated us from God and His presence has been done away with. Before the death of Jesus, a thick veil separated the Holy of Holies, the most holy place, from the rest of the world. It was in this room above the Ark of the Covenant where God "dwelt." Once a year, only the high priest could come in before the presence of God. In that day, you could not approach God's presence. It was only available to one man once a year. When Jesus died on the cross, paying for the sin of the world, the thick veil in the temple was supernaturally torn from top to bottom. The tearing of this veil was God declaring to the world that the sin problem separating us from Himself was now abolished once and for all by the cross of His Son. *"Therefore, brethren, having boldness to enter the Holiest by the blood of Jesus, by a new and living way which He consecrated for us, through the veil, that is, His flesh"* (Hebrews 10:19-20). God's presence is now available to all through Christ! We can approach Him and enjoy His presence.

Jesus did not just rend the veil to get us into the Holy of Holies someday, but to get the Holy of Holies into us now. *"Or do you not know that your body is the temple of the Holy Spirit..."* (1 Corinthians 6:19). In the time period before Jesus, people had to go to a certain place to worship God. If you wanted to worship God, you had to go to the tabernacle during Moses' lifetime or to the temple in Jerusalem after it was built in 957 B.C.

> *"And it shall be that whichever of the families of the earth do not come up to Jerusalem to worship the King, the Lord of hosts, on them there will be no rain"* (Zechariah 14:17).

People were accustomed to going to a specified location to worship and meet with God. This old covenant thinking still seems to reside in some of our mindsets today. Do we also feel that we need to go to a location, a church building, to worship and meet with God? That is not so anymore! Yes, it's vital to have fellowship with one another and to gather together (Hebrews 10:25). But it is very important we stop thinking that we need to go to a certain location to meet with God's presence. We no longer need to go to a building to worship and meet with God. The location is now in us. We are the place of meeting, the tabernacle of God's presence!

We have the greatest privilege that all the Old Testament prophets wished they could have had. We get to house the very presence of God Himself! We get to host the Holy Spirit of God. Everywhere we go now, the Holy of Holies goes with us. Sometimes we may think we need to get people to go to church so they can get saved or come to the altar for repentance. I have good news. Wherever we go, the altar of God goes with us. If you are in K-Mart or Wal-Mart, so is the very presence of God for the needs of others. Salvation, healing, deliverance or miracles are always available anytime, anywhere. YOU are a meeting place of God for yourself and for others.

Intimacy With God

Paul prayed, *"I keep asking the God of our Lord Jesus Christ, the glorious father that He may give you the spirit of wisdom and revelation so that you may know Him better"* (Ephesians 1:17 NIV). The main purpose of the veil being torn is to get up close and personal with God, to know God intimately. He is the object of our pursuit. Knowing Him intimately is our prize. *"Now this is eternal life that they may know you, the only true God, and Jesus Christ, whom you have sent"* (John 17:3). Eternal life is intimacy with God.

The word used in the Bible for know is *yada* (Hebrew) or *ginosko* (Greek). This type of knowing has little to do with an intellectual understanding of a subject. It is not a head knowledge type of understanding through scholastic study. This type of knowing is achieved through an intimate, deep, and up close relational experience. I could say I know President Obama, meaning I wrote a college essay on him and know some details about his life. But do I really know him? If I were at the White House, would he welcome me with open arms? No, he would not. In the same token, many know about God, but do not really know Him intimately, deeply and personally. If I told you that I know my children, it would mean that I really do know them. I *yada* or *ginosko* them. I could spend many hours telling you my fondest, funniest and impacting memories with them! Likewise, God wants us to know Him intimately. He wants us to experience Him and His kingdom up close and personal.

Heaven is Not Just a Future Attraction

It is important that we quit viewing the kingdom of heaven primarily as a future place of existence. Yes, we will experience a realm called heaven when we die, but there is an important truth that I want you to really grasp. Christ died not only to get us into heaven but to get heaven into us. The kingdom of heaven is fashioned to invade our world today. If we relate heaven as only a future event, we will miss out on accessing what is available to us now.

Let's pretend you had a wealthy uncle who left you one million dollars invested in twenty-five year maturation U. S. Treasury bonds. You were to receive one million dollars in twenty-five years. Knowing that, you dreamed up some great ideas and plans for how to use that money in the very distant future. Suppose the U. S. Treasury called you up tomorrow and said, "You no longer have to wait twenty-five years. The one million dollars is available to you right now." Would you tell them, "No, that's okay. I don't really need the money right now, and I really desire to learn the gift of patience, anyway." Of course not! I hope you would start using that money immediately toward the plans you had dreamed up to advance God's kingdom now. The good news is that we do not need to wait for heaven's treasury bonds to mature either. Heaven and its resources are available to you now to advance God's kingdom here on earth.

Heaven is Available Now

During my first ministry trip to a Hispanic youth group in 2008, I met a 13 year-old girl named, Corina. During the meetings she was trained in basic prophecy and healing. Corina stepped out and prophesied over her friend, praying for her back that was in pain. All the pain left. This was the first time Corina had prayed for healing or prophesied. When sharing testimonies, I still remember her response: "I can't believe I can do this. I thought I would have to be a Christian for many years and go to Bible college before I could do something like this. I just got saved a few weeks ago. This is awesome!" Corina was experiencing the fact that the kingdom of heaven was available to her now. She didn't have a waiting or trial period to pass. Neither do we.

MY SON BRANDON'S CREATIVE MIRACLE

My youngest son, Brandon, also got to experience the kingdom of heaven first hand while visiting me in class during my first year at BSSM. A former BSSM graduate, revivalist Chad Dedmon, was ministering to our class. Chad had prayed for my son who was 12 at the time. This is Brandon's account in his own words of what occurred that day.

"I was watching him grow legs out and I wondered if one of my legs was shorter than the other one. I walked over and had him pray for me. My right leg grew out a little bit. It felt like something grabbed my leg and stretched it out, like jello." After Brandon received prayer, Chad left. Other people showed up wanting prayer, but Chad was gone. One student called his visiting Norwegian friend, telling her to hurry to the room so she could receive prayer. This friend from Norway had been seeing a specialist for years, because her left femur bone was three centimeters shorter than her right femur bone. She rushed into the room hoping for her miracle, but was disappointed

---

because Chad had already left. The group of students pointed to my son Brandon and said, "You just had your leg grow out, so you should pray for hers to grow out."

At Bethel we are taught when a miracle happens to someone, it can easily be duplicated through that same person who received the miracle. It is based on the premise of Matthew 10:8, "Freely you have received so freely give."

Brandon had never prayed for anyone's healing before, but coerced by the excited group, he consented and began to pray for this girl's shorter leg to grow out. Here is what Brandon said:

"I started praying for her, and she said, 'Maybe it won't happen,' but it grew out…It was awesome! It was perfectly fine when she went back to the doctor." The friend of the Norwegian girl reported that when she returned home to Norway, her leg was X-rayed and both of her legs were now the exact same length! That day my son Brandon accessed the kingdom of heaven that had already been available to him.

"And He raised us up together, and made us sit together in the heavenly places in Christ Jesus" (Ephesians 2:6).

The word "raised" used here is past tense, not future. If you are born again, you are seated in heavenly places at this precise moment. It is normal for heaven to begin to start manifesting in our lives the second we are born again. At the very point in time that we believe in Christ Jesus, the kingdom of heaven is accessible to us.

Know God and Do Great Exploits

Do you know why I believe God chose Joshua to be the successor to Moses and lead the Israelites into the promise land? Here is a big clue.

> *"Inside the Tent of Meeting, the LORD would speak to Moses face to face, as one speaks to a friend. Afterward, Moses would return to the camp, but the young man who assisted him, Joshua son of Nun, would remain behind in the Tent of Meeting"* (Exodus 33:11 NLT).

Why would Joshua stay behind in the Tent of Meeting? I think it is because God's presence was still lingering in that tent long after Moses had left. Joshua truly loved and valued God's presence, apparently more than any of the others. He wanted to be where the presence of God was. This set Joshua apart from the others. In Exodus chapter 24, Joshua ascended up Mount Sinai with Moses toward God's presence. He got very close to the cloud of His glory for forty days, closer to God than any other man besides Moses. I believe that God saw Joshua's love for being close to His presence and that was a good reason for him to lead a generation of giant killers. I believe God picked Joshua to be His man of the hour because he was marked by God's presence.

> *"But the people who know their God shall be strong, and carry out great exploits"* (Daniel 11:32b).

How Much Do You Want?

Bill Johnson has powerful understanding in regard to cultivating God's presence and partnering with the Holy Spirit. I quote Bill, "The Holy Spirit lives in every believer, but He rests upon only a few. God will entrust to you His presence to the degree that you will jealously guard it. The Holy Spirit will rest upon you to the degree that you do not quench or grieve Him."

> *"In the year that King Uzziah died, I saw the Lord sitting on a throne, high and lifted up, and the train of His robe filled the temple."* (Isaiah 6:1).

The train of His robe illustrates His presence filling the temple, like a bride's wedding dress with a long train that follows her. As the bride walks down the aisle more and more of the train of her dress fills the runway. Likewise the train of God's presence was in the temple but more of it kept coming. The temple was filled with His glory, but more glory kept showing up. The presence of God was getting thicker and intensifying. It would be like smoke filling a room. There are degrees of the heaviness and magnitude of His presence.

We know that our body is the current temple of His presence. The Holy Spirit lives in every believer, but He will keep coming and filling us to greater degrees, depending on how we properly steward His presence and His friendship. The Bible records that the temple at one time was so full of His glory that the priests could not minister because of the intensity of His presence. *"The priests could not continue ministering because of the cloud; for the glory of the Lord filled the house of God"* (2 Chronicles 5:14). I picture the priests laid out on the ground, overcome by the Spirit of God.

Kathryn Kuhlman, a healing revivalist in the 1950s through

1970s, cultivated a great measure of the Holy Spirit's presence and power. Benny Hinn shares in his book, *Good Morning, Holy Spirit*, the impact Kathryn Kuhlman had on him as a young man. Benny was touched mightily and marked by God's presence in one of her meetings in 1973. Benny said that people standing in line for blocks would often start shaking under the power of God hours before her miracle services began. One time Kathryn Kuhlman was walking through the kitchen of a hotel to leave a businessmen's meeting. The cooks and servers in the kitchen all fell out onto the ground under the power and presence of the Holy Spirit. Kathryn had cultivated such a friendship and intimacy with the person of the Holy Spirit that He rested on her life in great measure. The Bible says God is no respecter of persons (Acts 10:34). If He did it for one person, He wants to do it for you too.

So the question is, how much of Him do you want?

These Men Have Been With Jesus

"When they saw the courage of Peter and John and realized that they were unschooled, ordinary men, they were astonished and they took note that these men had been with Jesus" (Acts 4:13 NIV).

What made these unschooled, ordinary men so courageous and different? It was because they had been with Jesus. They had spent time in His presence and the result was they became bold as lions. You become like whom you behold. Jesus is the Lion of the tribe of Judah. By spending time with Jesus these men began to take on His attributes.

Our first call in ministry is to the Lord Himself. *"And He went up on the mountain and called to Him those He Himself wanted. And they came to Him. Then He appointed twelve, that they might be with Him and that He might send them out to preach, and to have power to heal sicknesses and to cast out demons"* (Mark 3:13-15). Jesus called to Him those He wanted. The disciples came. He appointed the Twelve to be with Him. Then He sent them out to preach and to set people free. It is important to note that Jesus called the Twelve to be in His presence before he sent them out to preach.

Fill Me Up Again

"And suddenly there came from heaven a sound like a mighty rushing wind, and it filled the entire house where they were sitting. And divided tongues as of fire appeared to them and rested on each one of them. And they were all filled with the Holy Spirit and began to speak in other tongues as the Spirit gave them utterance" (Acts 2:1-4 ESV).

In Acts 2, the Holy Spirit arrived on the scene in awesome power, shook the Upper Room and anointed the fearful disciples with tongues of fire and great boldness. The once timid men and women, hiding in the Upper Room with the door locked because of fear, were now outside open air preaching to the multitudes. Filled with supernatural courage, boldness and power, Peter preached the good news of the kingdom and gave an altar call where 3,000 men were born again. What a night and day difference in these disciples after the Holy Spirit filled them!

In Acts 4, Peter and John were brought before the highest religious leaders of their day and were told not to speak or teach in the name of Jesus anymore. They prayed to God to give them even more boldness to proclaim and perform miracles in Jesus name.

> *"And when they had prayed, the place in which they were gathered together was shaken, and they were all filled the Holy Spirit and continued to speak the word of God with boldness"* (Acts 4:31 ESV).

Wait a minute. I thought the disciples were already filled. In Acts 2 it says they were filled. Then in Acts 4:4 it says they were once again filled. Why did they need to be re-filled between Acts 2 and Acts 4?

Our fuel in the supernatural is the presence of God. Filling up your car's gas tank one time will not last a lifetime. Cars burn gasoline. Being filled with the Spirit once will not last a lifetime either. We must refuel with the presence of the Holy Spirit. We use Holy Spirit power to minister to others. It is imperative that we continually refill and refresh our tanks in God's presence.

BE FILLED TO OVERFLOWING

> *"And do not be drunk with wine...but be filled with the Holy Spirit"* (Ephesians 5:18).

"Be filled" is the Greek word *pleroo*. It is a present tense verb, reflecting a continual sense. It literally means to "keep on being filled, to never quit being filled, to be continually filled." It is stating that we are to be endlessly filled with the Holy Spirit. We can never be too full!

In John 15, Jesus talks about abiding in the vine. John 15 says,

"I am the vine, you are the branches. If you strive and try really, really hard, you will bear a little piece of fruit." Oops, I was accidentally reading from the Universal Good Works translation. Okay, Jesus really says this, *"I am the vine; you are the branches. If you remain in me and I in you, you will bear much fruit"* (John 15:5). When we rest in His love, fruit will automatically happen. Jesus says much fruit will happen through rest, not through striving. It is more important to be filled with His love toward us than trying to produce fruit. As we focus our affections and thoughts on His presence, we will encounter His presence. The more we focus on abiding in His presence, the more of His presence will overflow to those around us and fruit of the kingdom will just naturally occur.

> *"One minute of God's presence can accomplish more than twenty years of your striving. Fruitfulness flows from intimacy."* – Heidi Baker

Psalm 23 says, *"You anoint my head with oil and my cup overflows."* Our assignment is to let the Holy Spirit continue to anoint our heads with oil until our cup is so full that it begins to overflow to those around us. Just imagine God's measure of the Holy Spirit as the river of God mentioned in Ezekiel 47. This river is an unending eternal supply of God's goodness ready to anoint us to overflowing. Picture this mighty, rushing river filling up a swimming pool, a container of limited supply, representing us.

What would happen to this swimming pool?

The pool would quickly fill up and then the abundant amount of water would spill over the edges. The entire ground that is in direct contact of the pool would soon be flooded. That is a great picture of what ministry can look like. As we spend time with God, we can be so full and overflowing with God's presence that we cannot help but splash His love and kingdom on everyone that comes into contact with us. We leave a squishy trail of His kingdom everywhere we go. There are puddles of miracles, signs and wonders following us in our presence-soaked footprints.

"These signs shall follow those that believe" (Mark 16:17).

WHICH WAY TO HEAVEN

We know that the kingdom of God is available now, but you may be thinking to yourself, "This all sounds great, but where is the kingdom of God and how do I get there?" Great question! Let me see if I can help. (Note: I will be using the kingdom of heaven and the kingdom of God interchangeably.)

There is a very important principle to help access the supernatural kingdom of God. You will hear it throughout this book. What we become aware of, we are able to experience. Let me say it again. It is that important. What we become aware of, we are able to experience. It is about becoming aware of the kingdom of God so that we can experience it. To become aware of this kingdom we need to know where it is located. We all know that when we die our spiritual body leaves our physical body, and our spiritual body goes to either heaven or hell depending on our relationship to Jesus. Right? So the kingdom of God or heaven must be a spiritual place and cannot be accessed by the physical realm. The kingdom of God has to be accessed and experienced by our spiritual man because it is a spiritual place.

"We are not human beings having a temporary spiritual experience; we are spiritual beings have a temporary human experience." – John Paul Jackson

We already have all of the supernatural equipment that we need. We already are a spiritual being living in a physical body having a soul. Our spiritual man is eternal and is fully equipped to hear and access the heavenly realms. One of the biggest keys to accessing and experiencing all that the kingdom of heaven has for us is to recognize that the kingdom of God is inside of you.

> *"The kingdom of God is not coming in ways that can be observed, nor will they say, 'Look, here it is!' or 'There!' for behold, the kingdom of God is within you"* (Luke 17:20-21 WEB).

The doorway to the kingdom of God is through your spirit. The Holy Spirit reveals things from heaven to your spirit. *"The Spirit himself bears witness with our spirit that we are children of God"* (Romans 8:16). The Holy Spirit gives us revelation and access to the kingdom of God through our spirit also referred to in scripture as our heart.

When I say heart, I am not talking about the physical heart muscle, but rather the unseen core of our being. I use heart and spirit interchangeably to talk about how we access and hear from the kingdom of heaven.

> *"I pray also that the eyes of your heart may be enlightened in order that you may know the hope to which he has called you, the riches of his glorious inheritance in the saints"* (Ephesians 1:8 NIV).

47

The eyes of your heart refers to the eyes of our supernatural understanding. It is spiritual in nature, not physical.

Say this slowly and out loud three times, and allow this truth to really sink in, "The kingdom of heaven is inside of me. The kingdom of heaven is inside of me. The kingdom of heaven is inside of me." Ponder on this truth. By learning to quiet our busy minds and our activities, we can start tuning into our heart and spirit to hear the voice of God. We will begin practicing God's presence and hearing His voice in the following chapters. How exciting is that!

HIGH SCHOOL FOOTBALL GAME BREAKOUT

At the beginning of my second year at BSSM, my friend, Jason Tax, and I decided it would be a great day to empty some wheelchairs. We set off to a nearby elderly mobile home park looking for handicap parking signs. After going door to door for hours we only got to pray for one elderly lady. She would not even open her locked screen door for us to pray. Completely discouraged that we didn't get to see the miracles I read about in Acts 3 of the lame man walking at the Gate Beautiful, we went home.

That night the Holy Spirit spoke to my heart, "Jason, what were you doing today?" I told Him we were going out to get what Jesus paid for. We wanted to see wheelchairs emptied! The Holy Spirit said, "Jason, you are trying too hard. When you're out in public, I want you to focus more on enjoying My presence being with you and loving people rather than focusing on emptying wheelchairs." I agreed, so the next day I decided to spend the day in my room getting to know the Holy Spirit better and enjoying His presence. Later that night Jason Tax asked if I wanted to join him in praying for people at the local high school football game. This time I was determined to focus more on enjoying God's presence with me rather than healing the sick. Here is the testimony I recorded that night:

When we arrived at the high school, my son, Brandon, saw one of his friends. We approached him and asked, "Would you like to feel God's presence?" He said, "Sure." We had him put the palm of his hands facing up and say, "Holy Spirit, come." When he did that, God's presence came. He started to laugh and he could hardly stand up. We had to hold him up to keep him from falling over. He said he felt happy and wobbly. *"In Your presence is the fullness of joy"* (Psalm 16:11). After we shared the Gospel of salvation with him, this young man asked Jesus into his heart!

Next, we saw a small group of teenagers, and a cheerleader in this group happened to move her sleeve up for Jason Tax to notice an ace wrap bandage on her wrist. Jason and I both had right wrist written down as something we felt God would heal that night. We approached the small group and told them about our healing list, and the cheerleader freaked out. She started telling all her friends about the healing list.

Before we knew it, more of their friends gathered around. We told them that if anyone had pain or needed healing to put that body part in the center of the group. They did as we asked and again we asked them to pray, "Holy Spirit, come." We told them to start moving their hurt body parts around and to check them out. The cheerleader was shocked and started tearing up as she shook her right wrist intensely, now pain free. Another cheerleader was overwhelmed in excitement as Jesus completely healed her right wrist also. Many teens got healed in that moment. We told them about this wonderful Jesus that healed them. We shared the Gospel and many of them got saved.

About that time the head cheerleading coach came over to us, checking out what was happening with her girls. The two cheerleaders that had just received their healing told the coach about the healing list and how Jesus healed their wrists. The cheerleading coach said she appreciated what we were doing, but she really needed her girls back on the field. After the cheerleaders left, we taught the remaining group how to experience the presence of God.

More teens started to become aware of God's presence. One girl was overcome with joy. She ran away to try to make the joy stop as she was laughing uncontrollably. She later came up and told us, "I felt wind, electricity and heat in my hands." These teens began going around finding their sick friends or anyone they felt needed healing. We had them pray for each other, As far as we could tell, every person was healed. They also brought to us anyone they thought needed a touch from God so that we could do "The Holy Spirit thing" on them. Other miracles happened in His manifest presence as they walked through a certain area where many healings had taken place. Without us even speaking a word. Yea, Jesus!

A third year BSSM intern named Anne Evans and some of

her friends joined in on the fun. They started to prophesy and pray for any needs these teens had. The high school youth started forming lines for Anne and her friends to pray and prophesy over them. I heard one teen boy referring to Anne say, "That lady right there told me everything that I have ever done. She even told me the kind of dog I have. Go have her tell you your future." Next, the cheerleading coach walked up to us and asked, "Before the game ends, can you come out to the field and pray over our entire cheerleading squad? We currently have a tremendous amount of injuries." I thought to myself, "Wow!" We told her that we would be honored to do that.

Many more healings, salvations and fillings of the Holy Spirit happened as teens kept coming. We had the youth that had just gotten saved and filled with the Holy Spirit pray for their sick friends and most of them were instantly healed. A young man with a broken foot was healed, walking off without his crutches. Headaches and sinus problems from colds were instantly healed. Pain left bodies. God fixed a girl's frozen finger that could not bend, as a security guard looked on.

At one point, I had to stop and look around. I wanted to take in this precious moment. Groups of teens were everywhere. They were in separate groupings inviting the Holy Spirit to come, praying for the sick and getting touched by His presence. The youth were holding each other up, trying to keep from falling over because God's presence was so heavy on them.

Before the game ended we found the cheerleading coach. She called all of her girls into a group huddle right on the sideline of the field in front of the grandstands.

The game was going on behind us as the coach explained to the girls who we were and asked us to pray for their healing. We asked them to put any body part that needed healing in the center of the huddle. Sound familiar? Knees with braces, hands wrapped up, and many ankles were all placed in the center of the group. We all invited, "Holy Spirit, come." I love the Holy Spirit! Jesus healed every one of them. "This is so weird. I can't believe this," the girls said after Jesus healed them. We asked the entire squad if they wanted to know this Jesus that healed them up close and personal. We shared the Gospel of salvation and all the girls' response was "Yes!"

The entire cheerleading team, in front of the grandstands, bowed their heads accepting Jesus as Savior. They all invited the Holy Spirit to radically fill them and set them ablaze. One of the girls mentioned having a shorter leg, so my friend, Jason, grabbed a chair and asked the cheerleading team to watch Jesus do another miracle. He had the cheerleading team pray as they watched her leg grew out about half an inch. The girl in the chair started crying and said, "I felt it grow out!"

After the game ended, we walked to our car. We noticed a small gathering of teens sitting on a block wall. We approached them and shared some of the miracle stories we had seen that night. One brash girl blurted out, "I am a pagan!" We told her, "That's okay. Jesus still believes in you, and He loves you just the same." We asked her if she wanted to feel God's presence. She said "No," then paused for a moment and changed her reply.

"Okay, sure." We asked her to hold her hands in front of her and say, (you guessed it) "Holy Spirit, come." She said she felt heat and tingling in her hands. We explained to her that she was experiencing God the Holy Spirit.

She told us that she had arthritis in her hands and a back problem. We prayed for her back and hands as she kept opening and closing her fists. She bent over to check her back and blurted out a string of four letter words from utter shock. After apologizing for her outburst, she said the knot that had been on her spine for years was now gone. Her hands felt totally loose and pain free. Two of her friends that were sitting on the wall also got healed. This outspoken girl experienced God's love and His presence personally. This entire group, prodded by this once "pagan" girl, all asked Jesus into their hearts. They all got saved!

A friend's daughter who attended this high school said everywhere she walked that night she heard students talking about the Holy Spirit. As she was leaving the game, she overheard a couple of her guy classmates talking to each other. One of them said, "Maybe the Holy Spirit could help you out with that problem."

Earlier that night while praying for a young man's broken arm, a girl said, "I am the principal's daughter, and I do not believe in miracles. My dad would not like what you are doing here!" We blessed her and kept praying for the young man's arm. He was in a cast and all the pain left his arm. The next Sunday morning at Bethel Church this girl, the principal's daughter, came forward to receive Jesus as her Lord and Savior!

PRAYER- *"Father, please give us the greatest value and honor for your presence. Let your presence be more important to us than any gift that we may receive. Jesus, help us steward your glory well. Holy Spirit, come into our lives with great love and power. Help us experience and understand the kingdom of heaven. Most importantly, we want to know you and enjoy you forever."*

ACTION STEP

- Watch Video #2 - The Kingdom of Heaven is Here

Chapter Three

PURSUING THE PRESENCE

"There is a difference between praying to God and experiencing God through prayer." - Madame Guyon

Experiencing God and His kingdom through prayer is the greatest joy in my life. Everything in our Jesus-walk is meant to flow from intimacy. There are countless ways to encounter God's presence and to experience Him. I like to worship, meditate on the Word, go on driving dates with God, park and talk to God, sit in my room with God, watch movies with the Holy Spirit, journal with Jesus...In fact, my whole life revolves around the awareness that God is with me all the time. In this chapter I focus on two modes of presence-prayer: soaking prayer and practicing God's presence.

These two methods of presence-prayer may be new to you, as they were to me a few years ago. What is significant about these methods of prayer is the goal of the prayer: To become aware of the presence of God. It is tuning our spiritual senses to experience His manifest presence.

CHASING THE CLOUD OF HIS PRESENCE

Our mission is being aware of and following God's presence. God's Spirit is continually moving, so it's valuable to discern, adjust and change directions to follow His presence if He moves. When I say that He has moved, I am referring to the sensing of His presence.

In Exodus 13, the children of Israel were led by God's visible presence. God's presence showed up as a cloud by day and a pillar of fire by night. When the cloud rested in a place, the children of Israel would stop, pitch their tents and camp there. When the cloud or pillar moved, the children of Israel knew it was time to pick up their tents to again follow God's tangible presence. How ridiculous it would have been for the Israelites to tell God, "No, God, I cannot move anymore. I am tired of all this change. I want to pitch my tent right here. There is a great view of Mount Sinai from this spot." Likewise, we are to be followers of God's presence and move when His presence does. If we feel like a certain aspect of our prayer life has seemed to dry up, maybe it is time to pick up our tent and change the way we pursue the cloud of His presence.

If we only know one way to pray and experience God's presence, what happens if He moves? We may incorrectly deduct that it's the season of dry wilderness for us. I believe that most seasons of dryness in our lives are when God's cloud moves and we do not. When His presence has seemed to move, it is our mandate to recognize that He has moved. It is time to pick up our tents and pursue God's presence in various ways until we find Him. If your normal prayer life has seemed to dry up, it is probably that He moved. It is our mission to follow the cloud of His presence. I will pursue Him in various ways and when I feel His presence, I will camp there. My focus is to find where His presence is and camp there to enjoy Him.

SEEK FIRST HIS KINGDOM

I used to intercede and petition God for all my urgent needs and the needs of others. This is fine, but I want to show you another way to bring your needs before God. Instead of fervently praying out loud for all my needs, I started resting in God's presence, letting my needs and desires be known to God in the silent communication of my heart. I made His presence the main focus of my prayer life, not my needs. *"But seek first His kingdom and His righteousness, and all these things will be given to you as well"* (Matthew 6:33). As I chose to do that, I noticed that He took care of all the other issues of my life. God already knows our needs. As we choose to spend time in His presence, He will many times answer the thoughts and desires of our heart. I encourage you to put His presence as your main purpose in your prayer life and see what happens.

When I was in my second year at BSSM, I was in silent prayer enjoying God's presence and I thought in my heart, "I really would like to go on a ministry trip with Kevin Dedmon, and I would really enjoy getting to minister on the streets with Chris Overstreet. That night I received an email from Kevin Dedmon inviting me to go on a ministry trip with Him. The very next day at Bethel Church, Chris Overstreet walked up to me and invited me to start ministering on the streets with him. I was shocked. God was teaching me that as I chose to put His presence as a number one priority in my life, He would take care of the rest. He would answer my innermost thoughts, concerns and desires. I was learning that intimacy in prayer is primarily about being in His presence. The presence of God, His face, is our greatest treasure.

Soaking Prayer

"In the silence of the heart God speaks. If you face God in prayer and silence, God will speak to you." – Mother Teresa

Soaking prayer is a prayer of stillness and quiet. This one form of prayer alone could radically jumpstart your spiritual life. As you learn to be still in God's presence, the awareness of His presence and His voice will increase in your life. For me, soaking prayer has been the greatest avenue to experience the manifest presence of God. If soaking prayer is the only thing you acquire from this book, I believe your life will be incredibly impacted. Practice soaking prayer until you can comfortably sit or lie in stillness in His presence to enjoy Him. His presence will impact you like nothing else can.

So how do I soak?

Set aside thirty minutes of uninterrupted time. Turn off your cell phone ringer and remove any distractions you may have during this time. This is a special time set aside to be refreshed by God's presence. Psalm 46:10 says, *"Be still, and know that I am God."* Sit or lie down in a quiet room in total silence or listen to soft worship music. I recommend that you start your soaking journey with soft music and earphones. This helps tune out distracting noises. While you are listening to soft music, turn your heart to the Lord in affection and adoration. Pay attention to any feelings or awareness you have of God's presence. We already discussed this principle: What we become aware of, we are able to experience. Remember the kingdom of heaven is inside of us. You are not trying to get Him to show up as much as you are practicing awareness of the presence that is already there.

Many times in my heart, I will silently start thanking God for what He has done in my life. I will say, "Thank you, Jesus, for giving your life for me." Then I will pay attention to any awareness of His presence. I may start to feel God's presence as a tingling sensation, power or peace. If I feel anything, even if ever so subtle, I will thank Him for what I am sensing. A thankful heart prepares the way.

Another kingdom principle in the supernatural is thankfulness. What you give thanks for will increase. When Jesus gave thanks for the few loaves and fish he had to feed the multitude, what happened? God increased what Jesus gave thanks for, and the loaves and fish multiplied. In the same way, when I am soaking, as I give thanks for the awareness of God's presence, it will usually intensify. If I give thanks for the tingling I feel in my fingertips, the presence of God will most likely increase. As I become aware of that increase in God's presence, I then turn my heart in thanksgiving to the Holy Spirit for touching my fingers. Then that tingling presence may increase to feel more like electricity on my fingers or it may start to move through my hand or into my body. I enjoy learning how to soak in the Holy Spirit's presence.

As you train your senses to become aware of Him, more things may start to happen. In time you may end up having a feeling of incredible waves of power coursing through your body. It may feel like you have been plugged into a light socket. The Holy Spirit may take you into visions or start speaking clearly to your heart. When I soak, my motive is to spend time with Him and to become aware of what He is doing. I do not know what He will do, but I position myself to be aware, thank Him and enjoy our time together. Soaking is not a time to petition Him with a list of our personal needs. It is simply a time set aside to enjoy each other's company.

Removing mental distractions is central to soaking prayer. If your mind seems very active or you keep having things you need to do that day pop up in your mind, picture a windshield wiper taking those thoughts and worries from your mind. Distractions in your mind can hinder you from hearing your heart or spirit. As these distractions come up, you can also picture yourself putting them into helium balloons. Just release these balloons to Jesus and let your mind be still in peace. He may give you answers to your problems during this time too. It probably will take some practice to be still in His presence. We are used to so much busyness and activity during our day. That is a main reason why I cannot over-empathize how much soaking prayer can radically impact your life.

When I first started soaking, I would often fall asleep, but after waking up I would feel very refreshed. As I practiced soaking regularly, I began to stay awake and would feel a tingling of God's presence resting on my body. The more I spent time enjoying His presence, the more intense His presence would come. Many times the electrical currents and waves of the Holy Spirit's power would overwhelm me. I learned that God's presence was like an ocean, with wave after wave of His presence. *"...All your waves and swirling tides have passed over me"* (Psalm 42:7).

I noticed as one wave of His presence would fade and lift, if I waited for another wave, another wave of His presence would arrive. This next wave would be more intense and lasted longer in duration than the previous one. I was learning to wade out into the deeper waters of His presence. Tears of joy would run down my face, as I was flooded with strong feelings of His love turned toward me. Through practice, soaking has become a foundational part of my prayer life. I have found that being still and turning my affection towards His presence in soaking has trained my senses to be more in tune to the person of the Holy Spirit.

SUMMER SUPERNATURAL ADVENTURE

During the summer of 2007, I spent hours every day absorbing His waves of presence. As I did that, His anointing seemed to increase in my life, as physical healings and miracles in the marketplace became more frequent. My room became charged with the tangible presence of God. I could feel a real electrical presence in the air of my bedroom. When I started to pray, an actual breeze would blow around in my room. I wanted to make sure it wasn't an air draft, so I taped up all the windows and vents with duct tape. As soon as I turned my heart to the Holy Spirit, a gentle wind would move around in my room. The Holy Spirit was showing up in a real way! Electrical hot spots arrived on the scene, too. I could run my hands through these hot spots and feel electrical shocks like pins and needles.

Although I couldn't see them, I now have learned those hot spots were, in fact, angelic presence.

During these extended soaking sessions the Lord started bringing me into trances like Peter had in Acts 10:10:

> *"...Peter went up on the housetop to pray, about the sixth hour. Then he became very hungry and wanted to eat; but while they made ready, he fell into a trance and saw heaven opened and an object like a great sheet bound at the four corners, descending to him and let down to the earth."*

A trance is a state of being the Lord puts you into in order to show you supernatural revelation. Many times it is like the in-between state you feel right before you fall asleep or wake up. Sometimes I experienced a deep heavy peace almost like I was sedated, and then the Lord spoke. Other times in these trances, the Lord would show me visions or speak very clearly to my heart.

I began having some out of body experiences during these soaking sessions. *"I was caught up to the third heaven fourteen years ago. Whether I was in my body or out of my body, I don't know--only God knows"* (2 Corinthians 12:2). The Holy Spirit on occasions took my spirit right out of my physical body. Once I was taken to heaven where Jesus met me. That one experience made everything this world has to offer pale in comparison to Him. In that encounter I was wrecked for Jesus alone.

My room became the most exciting and amazing spot on the entire earth for me. I was also going out to love on people three times a week, and God was moving out there in power. Even so I would race back home to get into my room to spend more time with the Holy Spirit. One time, my friends came over to visit me as I was in prayer. I opened my door to check on the noise, and my friends were staggering down the hallway. They were leaning up against the walls trying to reach my room. They said they could barely walk because of the presence that was radiating from my room.

That summer completely transformed my prayer life. I had encounters in His presence that marked my life forever. When I went out in public, people said they felt tingling, chills or electrical currents as I walked up to them. The person of the Holy Spirit increasingly overshadowed me as I spent time getting to know Him. The Holy Spirit became the most real and important Person to me. I continue today in my main life pursuit of growing in friendship with the Holy Spirit and His presence.

PRACTICING THE PRESENCE OF GOD
- BROTHER LAWRENCE -

"If I were a preacher, I would preach nothing but practicing the presence of God. If I were responsible of guiding souls, I would urge everyone to be aware of God's constant presence, if for no other reason because His presence is a delight to our souls and to our spirits." – Brother Lawrence

Brother Lawrence lived in a monastery in Paris in the 1600s. He is most remembered for his one main passion and purpose in life, practicing the presence of God. Brother Lawrence spent years learning how to train his mind and heart to be in continual awareness of God's abiding presence. Throughout his daily menial duties and tasks as a kitchen worker he practiced the presence of God. He learned how to never break the union of God's presence in his life. Brother Lawrence learned how to be aware of God's presence every second of every day. It is said that people would come from far away to watch Brother Lawrence peel potatoes just so they could experience the presence of God that surrounded him.[1]

> *"Rejoice always, pray without ceasing, in everything give thanks; for this is the will of God in Christ Jesus for you"* (1 Thessalonians 5:16-18).

Brother Lawrence learned how to pray without ceasing. He realized you could pray without words. This inner prayer of silence was an inner awareness of God's presence. It is cultivating intimacy with the presence of God, which is prayer.

THE PROCESS OF PRACTICING GOD'S PRESENCE

So how did Brother Lawrence do this? Like soaking prayer, Brother Lawrence would turn his heart in affection, in adoration and worship to the Lord. He trained himself to be aware of God's presence within him throughout his entire day. He would attempt to keep that awareness of God's presence as long as possible. When he noticed that situations and distractions in his day would interrupt his union and awareness of His connection to God's presence, he would repeat the process and start over by turning his heart in affection to the Lord until the awareness of God's presence returned. He trained himself to keep his heart united to the Lord's presence throughout the day so that eventually he had continual unbroken fellowship in his heart with God's presence every moment of the day. The awareness of God's presence was so strong around him. Others noted when they were in the presence of Brother Lawrence, they were in the very manifest presence of God Himself.

Have you ever been caught up in God's presence during worship? You feel so close and near to God. It seems like heaven has arrived and God is right there in front of you. Then all of a sudden something distracts you, maybe your phone vibrates or someone bumps you as they walk by. Perhaps you have a flashing thought of an upcoming bill that needs to be paid and you are completely taken out of the awareness of God's presence. What just happened to you? Did God get up and leave the building? No, you did. You left, because in your mind you checked out.

Learning to train our mind to stay focused on God and His presence is doable. The kingdom of heaven is inside us and activated by our focused adoration and attention. In order to stay in that place of continual awareness of His presence, we can to train our mind to be aware of the natural realm and the supernatural realm inside of us at the same time. It is multitasking at its best. We can train ourselves to practice the presence of God and be in unbroken fellowship with Him.

HOSTING THE PRESENCE WHILE BUSSING TABLES

I started practicing the presence of God like Brother Lawrence when I bussed tables at an Olive Garden restaurant. Since I didn't have to talk to many guests, I would focus on the presence of the Holy Spirit around me. I would be aware of Him as I wiped down tables and cleared dishes. With practice I soon learned how to multitask, being aware of His presence and being aware of my job at hand. I felt as if my best friend was at work with me.

There were times when the Holy Spirit would tell me that I needed to go to a different section in the restaurant, because there were three tables that needed cleaned. When I got there, sure enough there were three tables that needed my attention. It took some practice, but it was a training ground for me. At times I felt so much of His presence and nearness as I cleaned off tables. Those days were glorious! A few customers even stopped at the front to talk to the manager about me saying, "There is something special about that busser you have. I have never seen anyone bus tables like him." I did not talk to those guests. I only cleaned off tables as I focused on feeling God's nearness in my heart. A letter was also mailed to the restaurant from an out-of-town guest telling the managers how great of a busser she thought I was.

The only thing I did was practice focusing on the presence of the Holy Spirit with me as I washed tables. The presence with me caused a supernatural favor the guests recognized and were drawn to. It was the Holy Spirit's presence on me.

How much of His presence do you want?

Moses was in the intensity of God's presence for forty days until his face shown. Jesus was in the presence of God's glory and

He was transfigured. Time spent in God's presence will change us!

ENDNOTES

1. *The Practice of the Presence of God* by Brother Lawrence
    (Benton Press, 2013)

 **ACTION STEP**

- Watch Video #3 – Soaking Prayer Activation

- Journal your experience

Chapter Four

God is Hiding to Be Found

"It's not about standing up and being an eloquent speaker. It's about being so close to the heart of God that you know what He's thinking. Then you're not afraid to go anywhere and say anything. The Lord Himself will do anything for radical lovers." – Heidi Baker

As we draw close to God and spend time with Him, He draws close to us and speaks to us in His spiritual language. *"Draw near to God and He will draw near to you"* (James 4:8). This type of communication is called the language of the Spirit. Sometimes this language of the Spirit can seem mysterious and unclear. God may show us pictures or give us information that we don't quite understand and grasp in the moment. That is very normal. Even Daniel, who had some of the most amazing encounters with God, took some time to sort out the meaning behind his experiences for understanding. *"I heard, but I did not understand..."* (Daniel 12:8 ESV).

God is Spirit (John 4:24). We, too, are spiritual beings having spiritual senses, just like we have natural senses. We have spiritual thought, touch, taste, sight, hearing and smelling. When God speaks to us, many times He will not speak to us in a natural spoken language such as English, French or German. God speaks to us at many times and in different ways (Hebrew 1:1). He communicates using His Holy Spirit speaking to our spirit (Romans 8:14).

LANGUAGE OF THE SPIRIT

I believe God is consistently communicating with us in some way, shape or form. One of His names, The Word, even reflects his ample desire for communication. If we do not understand His language of communication, then we will have a communication gap, not being able to recognize and comprehend when He is speaking to us. Flowing from God's creativity, the language of the Spirit consists of many things besides words.

Here are some common ways that God may speak: Visual pictures, random emotions, unusual coincidences and dreams, to name a few. We will discuss these in greater detail in the next chapter. This language of the Spirit can easily be missed if we do not recognize what to look for. Before I attended BSSM I thought the only ways God spoke to me was through reading my Bible and the Sunday morning sermon. Both of these are really important ways God does speak, but now I know of many more ways that He communicates. This is what I am excited to share with you. Hearing and recognizing His voice is a most exhilarating adventure.

RETRAINING OUR SPIRITUAL SENSES

To hear His voice we must retrain our spiritual senses. From the moment we are born, we are trained to receive revelation from the natural outside world through our five natural senses of sight, hearing, taste, smell and physical touch. That is our natural man. We also have a spiritual man with spiritual senses, and we need to practice receiving revelation from our spirit man. The natural realm is receiving information from the outside world. The spiritual realm is mostly receiving revelation from the inner man, your spirit.

Have you ever thought about a friend that you haven't seen in years, and then all of a sudden you cross paths and make contact with this person within a few days? You even tell them, "I was just thinking about you last week." You probably didn't associate thinking about them and then running into them as a supernatural encounter, but it was. You had a random thought and coincidentally saw them. That encounter was not just random but very supernatural. This is how the language of the spirit is many times, subtle and seemingly coming from your thoughts.

Have you ever daydreamed and then it came to pass? Again we have labeled it as mere coincidence, but the truth is we are spiritual beings receiving revelation from our spirit. The Holy Spirit will breath revelation on our hearts and minds, and many times it feels like our minds are wandering to a random subject. The Holy

Spirit is very much influencing these subtle thought shifts. With practice we can perceive this supernatural information and discern the Holy Spirit's language. The language of the Spirit can also seem like a riddle or a puzzle, and we need to put all the pieces together to understand what God is speaking to us.

THE GLORY IS IN THE SEARCH

Proverbs 25:2 says, *"It is the glory of God to conceal the word, and the glory of kings to search out the speech"* (Douary-Rheims Bible). This Bible verse states that God may conceal or hide His message for us to find; it's to a king's glory to find out what God is saying. We are His kings and priests.

It is similar to when we were children, waking up on Easter Sunday. We excitedly got out of bed, grabbed our little woven baskets, and launched out to search for all the hidden treasures. Do you remember those good times? So much of the excitement and adventure for both the children and parents was in the hiding, searching and finding.

How much fun would it have been to have awakened on Easter morning, only to discover that your father had done all the searching and finding for you already. Lo and behold, all the eggs were neatly and orderly stacked up, colored-coded in your basket for you next to your bed. He had even been kind enough to take it one step further and had lovingly opened all the eggs for you, putting all the little treasures that were inside the eggs neatly on your bed. Now it was much easier for you to enjoy all your treats without any searching or effort on your part. How would you like that? How much fun would that be? Not much fun at all!

The fun of the adventure is in the search.

In the same way uncovering and discovering what God is saying through the various ways He communicates to us is meant to be a great adventure. God gives us riddles and clues so we can enjoy the process of finding the treasure of what He is saying to us. He hides messages for us to find and interpret. This was a key to Daniel's success. He learned the language of God's Spirit and was sought after to solve God's riddles. "...*Because an excellent spirit, knowledge, and understanding to interpret dreams, explain riddles, and solve problems were found in this Daniel*" (Daniel 5:12). We, too, can learn to recognize and understand God's language of the Spirit.

This may all be new to you, but it is a fun escapade getting to uncover what God is speaking to us. I pray your walk with Jesus will be greatly encouraged in this chapter as you begin to recognize how much your loving Father is communicating His great love to you.

HIDE AND SEEK

God likes the adventure of playing hide 'n seek. He is hiding somewhere to be found by you. Banning Liebsher of Jesus Culture says, "God doesn't play hide 'n seek like teenagers do. A teenager's motive and goal is to never be found. They will go to great lengths and feats to not be found. Unlike a teenager, God isn't digging a hole in the back yard and covering Himself up with army camouflage to stay hidden at all cost. No! God is hiding to be found! God is like a father playing hide 'n seek with his four-year-old. The father purposely has his leg sticking out from behind the couch, kicking it up and down trying to catch the eye of his child. He is hiding for only one reason, to be found by his child! If he has to, he will even make enough noise to make sure that he is found. The joy of the father and the child is in the moment of being found." That is how our heavenly Father hides for us to be found.

Recognizing His presence and His voice may take some time and some practice, so be patient and give yourself ample amounts of grace for the process. We have lived most of our lives receiving information from the outside natural realm using our five natural senses. Now we are learning how to receive information on the inside from our spiritual senses. This is a life-long adventure of learning, activating and understanding how these spiritual senses work in us. Each person is different and God works with the individual. Don't compare yourself and your journey into the supernatural with anybody else. Instead, allow the amazing person of the Holy Spirit to individually guide you into all truth. Your spiritual senses will become more activated and trained with practice (Hebrews 5:14).

THE RHEMA WORD

"So then faith comes by hearing, and hearing by the word (rhema) of God" (Romans 10:17).

The Greek word rhema means the "spoken word of God." It is not referring to the written Scriptures of the Bible; that is the Greek word graphe, meaning "the written Scripture." The supernatural language of the Spirit is the rhema word of God, which helps build our intimacy in recognizing His voice.

It is vital to know the written Scriptures. We also need continual encounters with God's rhema spoken word. Listen to what Paul the apostle says, *"I want you to know, brothers, that the gospel*

I preached is not something that man made up. I did not receive it from any man, nor was I taught it; rather, I received it by revelation from Jesus Christ" (Galatians 1:12). Paul knew and memorized the Scriptures. He was a Pharisee of Pharisees, but he needed a face-to-face encounter with God's presence and Person. Paul needed a revelation from Jesus Christ with the rhema word of God. He had an encounter, a revealing of Jesus Christ Himself through supernatural experiences. Like Paul, we also have supernatural encounters waiting for us. He is hiding to be found, so let's go find Him.

CARISSA COMES OUT OF A COMA

We were on a Treasure Hunt and had just left the Indian Casino, when we noticed the Honda Accord in front of us had a peace symbol on the back window. A peace symbol was a clue we had on our treasure map. That was our signal to follow this car to see where this adventure might lead. At the stoplight, I ran up to the car, knocked on the window and asked the lady inside if she needed prayer for anything. The lady said with tears in her eyes, "I have to talk to you! Can you pull over?" When she pulled over, we saw big writing on her passenger side window that said, "PLEASE PRAY FOR CARISSA." This lady was Carissa's grandmother. She said Carissa was at UC Davis Hospital, dying from a drug overdose and had been in a coma for some time. The doctors had told the family to start making funeral arrangements and plans to get Carissa body home.

We told Carissa's grandmother that we felt like this was a divine appointment. We asked if there was any way we could drive down to UC Davis to pray that Carissa would wake up. She

---

arranged for us to drive down the next day to pray for her. When we walked into the ICU room to pray, we were not expecting to see what we saw. The doctors had removed a fourth of Carissa's skull to relieve pressure from the brain aneurism. The entire left side of Carissa's brain was exposed for us to see.

We prayed, worshiped Jesus and prophesied destiny over her. We didn't see any immediate results in Carissa's condition. We ministered to Carissa's family, and her mom gave her life to Jesus in the parking lot during lunch. We drove home, and two days later we received this text message from Carissa's dad, "Carissa just woke up from her coma!" Yea, Jesus!

Months later, Chris Overstreet asked if I would join him and a team to go to Bruce Street in Anderson, a nearby town south of Redding. Chris said that he had a dream of Bruce Street recently and wanted to follow the language of the Spirit. As we walked around the apartment complexes, we asked the Holy Spirit for specific details of what was going to happen there. I felt like a young lady was going to have a powerful, life-changing encounter. My friend Kyle said he saw the number 32 in his mind.

We walked to a random apartment complex on Bruce Street. Our team passed by several closed apartment doors and one particular door happened to be open. This door had a thick metal screen so we couldn't see inside the apartment. Chris knocked on the screen and said, "Does anybody in there need prayer?" A voice came back, "No, we don't need any prayer." We started to move on and my left knee started feeling strange. I felt I was to go back to that same door we had just left. I stood in front of the screen trying to glance inside, but couldn't make out anything because it was bright outside and darker in the apartment.

I said, "Hi, I know you just said you didn't need any prayer, but does anyone in there have a bad left knee?" A man's deep voice replied, "What are you doing?" I thought he was irritated, because I had come back and was now really bothering him. I said, "I just felt a pain in my left knee and thought it may mean that someone here has pain in their left knee." The man responded, "Jason, what are you doing?" I was confused that he knew my name. Then the screen door flung open. It was Carissa's dad! I was so happy to see him. We hugged, and I introduced them to Chris and Kyle. He invited us in and asked if I wanted to see Carissa. I said, "Yes! Is she here?" He told me that she lived in the same apartments! As we were waiting, Kyle got a supernatural clue for Carissa's stepmom's back. He prayed for her, and her back pain left.

After a few minutes, Carissa came though the front door in a motorized wheelchair. Her dad said, "Carissa, I want you to meet someone. This is Jason. He is one of the people that came down and prayed for you when you were in the coma." She opened her arms wide for me to come and hug her. As we embraced tears flowed freely from both of us. We cried tears of joy together. It was such a powerful moment of seeing God's goodness and love that had touched her life so powerfully.

She had given her life to Jesus since the coma and was now a lover of God. We shared a lot of stories together. Then we asked why she had to be in the wheelchair. A stroke caused by the brain aneurism caused the right side of her body to suffer paralysis. She had no movement and feeling in her right leg. We shared with Carissa that God not only wanted her to come out of the coma, He wanted her to be completely healed and restored. We prayed for Jesus to touch her. She started to feel tingling in her toes and she was able to wiggle them around for the first time. She slowly started to move her right foot around just a little bit. We lifted her up from the wheelchair to see if she could stand on her own. She could not. God was obviously doing something in her body, but that was all we got to see in the moment with her paralyzed condition. We all embraced and said our goodbyes for then.

When we stepped out the front door, I noticed that the apartment number had fallen off the wall. I asked Carissa's dad what the apartment number was. They said, "It is apartment number 32." Go figure! God is just so amazing. A couple months later, I was in Los Angeles on a missions trip. Chris Overstreet called me with lots of excitement in his voice. "We just bumped into Carissa again. Jason, guess what? Jesus has healed her! She is out of that wheelchair and she is walking. We laughed, cheered and gave Jesus loud shouts of joy for what He did for Carissa!

This is an amazing example of the language of the Spirit: A series of supernatural puzzle pieces all fitting together to create something truly wonderful. God is so creative in how He communicates with us. In the next chapter we discuss and practice receiving supernatural revelation from God.

ACTION STEP

- Watch Video #4 – Dream Journal Activation

Chapter Five

Supernatural Revelation

"For God speaks in one way, and in two, though man does not perceive it. In a dream, in a vision of the night, when deep sleep falls on men, while they slumber on their beds, then he may speak in their ear." – Job

We will now uncover some of the diverse ways that God speaks to us and how we receive that revelation. Like we discussed in the previous chapters, God's language can be similar to putting together a puzzle or solving a riddle. This chapter focuses on receiving heavenly information called revelation. Revelation can be simple mental images or profound heavenly visitations.

Regardless of how the revelation is received, it all comes from the same source. A quick inner impression that is from heaven can be just as powerful as an angelic visitation. It all originates from God and His kingdom and should be highly valued.

The Bible

"Some people like to read their Bibles in the Hebrew; some like to read it in the Greek; I like to read it in the Holy Spirit." – Smith Wigglesworth

When reading the Bible, pay attention to verses that seem to stand out or have more life on them. Ask the Holy Spirit questions as you read His Word. God loves to speak to us through His written Word. The Word of God is the truest, most reliable prophecy (1 Peter 19-21). Every encounter we have should be in agreement with God's nature according to the written Word of God. Not everything we see or experience will be in the written text of the Scriptures, but our experience must line up with the teachings of the written Word. Take, for example, if I had a dream that I was giving out McDonalds' hamburgers to the homeless. McDonalds' hamburgers are not mentioned anywhere in the Bible, but feeding the poor is. For that reason, I could come to the conclusion that this dream was probably God speaking to me about doing something to feed the poor. Any experiences or interpretation of revelation must follow sound Biblical truths.

Unusual Coincidences

God speaks through random reoccurring coincidences. So pay attention to these events. I started to recognize these random unusual coincidences during the night while I was in first year BSSM. I would be awakened by a series of knocks on my bedroom door at random times in the night. When I went to the door, nobody was there and my housemates were all asleep. When I asked them in the morning if they had heard the knocking, they said they had not. A friend told me that sometimes God will wake us up at a specific time in the night because the time on the clock will references a certain Bible Scripture. He is communicating with us through the time depicted on the clock. After being made aware of this, whenever I heard knocking, I awoke and looked at the clock and recorded that time. I would ask the Holy Spirit which book in the Bible to reference the time with, and then I would look it up. God would use these times to powerfully communicate a Bible Scripture to me.

For about a year, almost on a daily basis I have been seeing the numbers 1038 and 316. Most often for me, it's when I glance at a clock or my cell phone and the time is 10:38 or 3:16. Many times I have awakened and looked at the clock and it was 3:16 a.m. One Thanksgiving night, I was getting up for a midnight snack at a little after 1:00 a.m. I walked downstairs and the microwave time was incorrectly showing 3:16 a.m. In those instances, I know that God is speaking to me. These two Scriptures, John 3:16 and Acts 10:38, are two of my primary life verses. They speak to me about my calling to become love to others and move in power.

> *"For God so loved the world that he gave his one and only Son, that whoever believes in him shall not perish but have eternal life"* (John 3:16 NIV).

"How God anointed Jesus of Nazareth with the Holy Spirit and power, and how he went around doing good and healing all who were under the power of the devil, because God was with him" (Acts 10:38 NIV).

INTERNAL KNOWING

This is a gut feeling, an internal knowing. They used to call this an unction. It is a pulling on your spirit by the Holy Spirit. Sometimes, you feel compelled and pulled to do something or say something to someone although in your natural mind it makes no rational sense. You may say something like, "I don't know why, but I just feel like I am supposed to contact this old friend of mine." When you do contact them, you see the Lord's hand on it and many times that old friend has been thinking about you too. The Holy Spirit was pulling on your spirit to reveal something.

Other times it is like "you know that you know that you know." But you can't explain how you know it. The world calls it ESP but in the Holy Spirit it is a supernatural perception. Sometimes when God is warning you of danger, you will "feel" that something is just not right. Pay attention to these internal impressions.

"And immediately, when Jesus perceived in His spirit that they reasoned thus within themselves, He said to them, 'Why do you reason about these things in your hearts?'" (Mark 2:8).

PHYSICAL IMPRESSIONS

Physical impressions seem to be felt on your physical body. You will feel God's presence as a sensation on a specific body part such as a heaviness or weight, pain, heat, tingling, pressure, a cool breeze, a vibration, electricity or some other manifestation. God may give us these physical impressions to communicate that He wants to heal someone. If my left shoulder starts to hurt all of a sudden with no prior history of a left shoulder problem, I would realize that God was informing me that someone has a bad left shoulder and He desires to heal it. These impressions will sometimes feel like a sympathy pain and you will be able to describe exactly the pain someone else has in their body. They may come on you when you ask the Holy Spirit to give you insight or it may catch you by surprise as you are going about your day. A Holy Spirit physical impression might hit you on a certain body part. That is when you are able to stop and ask the person by you if they have a problem in that particular body part. If they do, you are available to minister healing to them.

HEALING A BROKEN HEART

One day I was walking by a tattoo shop downtown. As I walked by three young men sitting on some stairs, my heart physically started to hurt with a sharp pain. It was so painful that I almost lost my breath. I asked the Holy Spirit, "What is this all about?" I felt He said this impression was not for a physical healing, but one of the young men's hearts was hurting from a broken relationship. I turned back around and asked the three young men if the information I felt made sense to them. They all flipped because they were meeting together specifically to cheer their friend up who had just gotten dumped by his girlfriend of a couple years. This young man realized how much God loved him and how real He was in that moment. Each of the young men wanted a deeper relationship with this personalized Jesus and they recommitted their lives to following Him. They felt God's tangible presence on their bodies as we prayed for the Holy Spirit to fill them.

Emotions and Feelings

God uses our emotions and feelings to communicate with us. Let's say you walked into a hair salon and you were in your normal emotional state. Once inside, a continual anxiety of fear about bills and lack of money kept hitting your emotions. You felt pressure and stress about how you were going to pay your bills even though you are not facing this problem in your own life. This random emotional state is a way the Holy Spirit would be letting you know somebody in that salon is feeling very stressed about their finances. It may be the business owner, a customer or an employee. You can then ask the Holy Spirit to show you who it is for and what He wants you to do about it. In chapter eight we will be discussing several ways to approach and minister to others in public.

The Still, Small Voice

The still, small voice of God usually comes as a thought or series of thoughts. Sometimes it is hard to distinguish whether these thoughts are coming from you or from God. Continuing in the practice of quiet prayer helps us to become aware and recognize the still, small voice of God. If I get a thought that is really random and seems to come out of left field, I will pay close attention to it.

Let's say I am having lunch with some friends and all of a sudden I start thinking about diabetes. That random thought would catch my attention, so I would ask my friends, the waitress or anyone nearby that seemed to stand out if they happen to have diabetes. I have seen God do mighty things through His still, small voice.

> *"The Lord said, 'Go out and stand on the mountain in the presence of the Lord, for the Lord is about to pass by.' Then a great and powerful wind tore the mountains apart and shattered the rocks before the Lord, but the Lord was not in the wind. After the wind there was an earthquake, but the Lord was not in the earthquake. And after the earthquake a fire; but the Lord was not in the fire: and after the fire a still small voice"* (1 Kings 19:11, 12).

In this encounter God was not in the wind, earthquake or the fire. This time He spoke to Elijah with His still, small voice.

THE INNER AUDIBLE VOICE

This is a clear sounding voice that seems to come from inside of you. It may sound very quiet or loud to you, almost thundering loud, but others around you won't hear it because it comes from inside you. It will leave a strong impact on you. It is a supernatural voice spoken to your spirit.

NEW NAME ON A WHITE STONE

The first time I heard God speak to me in this way was when I was learning how to do soaking prayer. I was in the Bethel

---

prayer chapel trying to soak and in no time I was snoring. In my sleep a mighty, deep pitched voice thundered out, "JEDIDIAH!" I did not know anyone by that name. That roaring voice shook me and I was awakened from a deep sleep. I was startled and my whole body inside seemed to be vibrating. It was a similar experience to someone running into your bedroom when you were fast asleep and yelling, "WAKE UP!" It had that kind of startling impact. I didn't know what had just happened. Never hearing that name before, I wrote Jedidiah in my notebook thinking maybe I would meet him later for a divine encounter.

Months later in a prophetic encounter, I saw a vision of the name Jedidiah written on a white stone and then God handed it to me. The Holy Spirit disclosed to me that the name Jedidiah is a name that God calls me. Revelation 2:17 speaks about God giving out white stones with new names written on them. I looked up the significance of the name Jedidiah and it means "Beloved of the Everlasting." This series of Jedidiah events has strengthened my identity as being a beloved son of my everlasting Father in heaven.

> *"And I will give him a white stone, and on the stone a new name written which no one knows except him who receives it"* (Revelation 2:17).

THE OUTER AUDIBLE VOICE

This is a voice you can hear in the physical realm with your natural ears. Others can hear the sound too, although they may not perceive what was said. What happened at Jesus' water baptism is a great example of this.

> *"Then a voice came from heaven, saying, 'I have both glorified it and will glorify it again.' Therefore the people who stood by and heard it said that it had thundered. Others said, 'An angel has spoken to Him.' Jesus answered and said, 'This voice did not come because of Me, but for your sake'"* (John 12:28-30).

It is interesting that what the Father spoke was not for Jesus' sake, but it was for the sake of the people. Even then, they didn't perceive what the Father was saying. Look at what I believe the Bible says about why they couldn't understand what was said to them in that incredible encounter.

> *"Hearing you will hear and shall not understand, and seeing you will see and not perceive; for the hearts of this people have grown dull"* (Matthew 13:14-15).

Having a childlike heart to hear and receive things from His kingdom is key to hearing and seeing in the spirit. *"Unless you become (change and repent) as a child you will in no means enter the kingdom"* (Matthew 18:3). Receiving heavenly revelation in a childlike manner is important. God has given us a brain to use but sometimes our rational brain can get in the way of receiving revelation. Revelation must be grasped by a childlike heart of faith.

OPEN VISIONS

Open visions appear as if they are being viewed with your natural eyes. But they are in fact your spiritual eyes that are seeing in the spiritual realm. You can't tell the difference in the moment because what you are seeing looks so real, just as if your natural eyes were viewing it. Once an angel suddenly appeared in my living room. I screamed loudly from fear and panic. Now I understand why angels in the Bible often announce their arrival with the words, "Do not be afraid." In the moment it seemed like the angel was being viewed through my natural eyes, even though it was a spiritual experience.

Most often others around you won't see what you are seeing, unless they are having the same supernatural encounter. Open visions can appear as if you are watching a supernatural movie screen right before your eyes. Our pastor, Kris Vallotton, had an open vision one day at the beach. A movie type screen appeared above a young man's head that he didn't know. Kris was able to describe all the scenes in detail that he was viewing. God was showing Kris this young man's entire life as it passed before his eyes. This young man, along with Pastor Kris, was shocked in this experience and both had a radical God encounter that day.

Brittney at Applebee's

One day I was at Applebee's restaurant with some friends eating lunch, and I looked out the window and saw another friend that wasn't expecting to be joining us. She was walking through the parking lot to the restaurant. At that moment I said, "Look! Brittney is coming to eat lunch here too." Then her image vanished and I realized God had just given me an open vision. About thirty minutes later, Brittney did, in fact, walk into this restaurant. Upon seeing us there, she decided to join us for lunch. I was given a supernatural vision from the Holy Spirit showing me things to come.

"However, when He, the Spirit of truth, is come, he will guide you into all truth: for he shall not speak of himself; but whatever he shall hear, that shall he speak: and He will show you things to come" (John 16:13). Another translation says, *"He will tell you the future."*

INNER VISIONS

Inner visions appear in the eyes of your imagination, the screen of your mind. If I said to you, "Okay, close your eyes and picture a sandy beach in Hawaii, palm trees blowing in the wind and a white hammock swaying back and forth," you most likely would be able to see that beautiful Hawaiian scene on the backdrop of your mind. Take a moment to close your eyes and try to picture this Hawaiian beach scene in your mind. Can you see it? It may appear subtle or clear. God will often use this screen of our mind to give us supernatural insights.

Now take a moment, close your eyes, and try to picture the very first childhood memory that you can recollect. Try to see it on the screen of your mind. Okay, now try to see if you can observe a memory that is even earlier. The way you are viewing these childhood memories on the screen of your mind is the same way God gives us prophetic images for people. The Holy Spirit will place images on that same screen that you viewed the Hawaiian beach and remembered your earliest childhood memories. These images can be subtle and vague or clear and sharp. They may appear as a still picture like a snapshot, or they can be a stream of pictures like watching an internal movie. These impressions on the screen of your mind can be very powerful for ministry. The Lord will often use visions along with physical impressions and His still, small voice at the same time to communicate His desire to heal people.

EAR BONES GROW BACK / TUMOR DISSOLVES

During the ministry time in a Southern Californian church, Jesus was there in power. I believe we witnessed over one hundred miracles that weekend. We saw seven deaf ears open, a wheelchair emptied and so many incredible miracles of God's goodness and love. We remain novices, but the Holy Spirit is not. He is very good at what He does! One young man had no inner ear bones in his left ear. A disease called Meningitis had eaten them away, making it physically impossible to hear. He had not been able to hear in that ear for several years. After praying for him, he could hear whispers in that deaf ear. He started weeping when he realized what God had done for him. God had recreated new ear bones!

I was calling out body parts as I would feel impressions on my body, saying things like, "God is healing a left shoulder; move it around!" Then I heard the Holy Spirit speak to my heart that He was going to heal a lady's tumor. Immediately I saw a very quick inner image of under a lady's left arm. I declared, "Jesus is healing a lady's tumor under her left arm. Go check to see if it is gone!" A lady with a tumor under her left arm came up to tell me that when I spoke that word out, she went to the bathroom and looked for the tumor. It had totally disappeared!

SMITH WIGGLESWORTH

Once as I was praying for a lady, I looked at her face and it changed before my eyes to be the face of the great healing evangelist, Smith Wigglesworth. It looked as though her face was morphing back and forth from her face to his. In that moment, I understood that the Holy Spirit was giving me this vision because He wanted me to prophecy and declare over her that she would have faith like Smith Wigglesworth. She told me later that God had asked her a couple weeks prior to start reading and studying the life of Smith Wigglesworth, so that she could grow in faith. She had already planned on buying his books. God used this supernatural vision to confirm and encourage her to study Wigglesworth's life for an impartation of great faith.

DREAMS

"Now when they had departed, behold an angel of the Lord appeared to Joseph in a dream, saying, Arise, take the young Child and His mother, flee to Egypt, and stay there until I bring you word; for Herod will seek the young Child to destroy Him" (Matthew 2:13).

Dreams are a common way that God speaks. Some of the most important messages that God has spoken to mankind have been through dreams. Everyone has dreams even if they do not remember them once they awake. Place a journal by your bed and then pray like Samuel, "Speak, Lord, your servant is listening." When you awake in the morning, even if all you can remember is an image of a blue car, write it down. Before long you will be able to remember and record more details of your dreams. You will see that God is speaking to you in the night. Three years ago, I did not remember any of my dreams. Now I usually record a dream every night. I do notice that if I start to decline in writing my dreams down, I remember fewer details when I awake.

In many dreams, God speaks symbolically through colors, shapes, numbers and other details. Your dreams might not make sense unless you unpack the revelation of the symbolism. I recommend getting a dream interpretation book from John Paul Jackson. This will be a great tool for you. It can help you decipher what God might be saying to you through the symbolization. However, always ask the Holy Spirit first what these symbols mean in your dream, because He may be saying something very personal to you that wouldn't be printed in a generalized book.

Many happenings in the kingdom of God rely on us being good stewards of what God has already given to us. When we steward the gifts of God well, we will be set up for a greater increase (See Matthew 25:14-30). I encourage you to steward your dreams well. You will be greatly blessed if you do. Place a notebook and pen next to your bed. Ask God to speak to you in your dreams and help you remember them when you awake. Once you awaken, write down everything you remember. Use a dream guide to interpret the dreams with the Holy Spirit. You will be largely encouraged in doing this. You will uncover many wonderful messages that God is communicating to you through your dreams.

LOVE IS BLIND

I had a dream that my friend Sean was singing, "Love is blind. You need to come see for yourself." When I awoke I felt the Holy Spirit say, "Today you will meet a blind man, and I am

---

going to heal him." That morning we met a man named Doug that was seventy percent blind. He had three eye diseases, and the doctors had told him that he would be completely blind in a short amount of time. He had big dark glasses and a white cane. We prayed for him three times and Jesus healed him! He read the smallest of print and signs on buildings as clearly as I could. Doug looked up toward the sun without his glasses and said he experienced no pain. He said he had not been able to do that before we had prayed. Doug said, "When I woke up this morning, I knew something good was going to happen to me." Handing us his white cane he said, "I won't need this anymore." I believe Doug was the first case of blindness I personally saw healed.

OTHER WAYS THAT GOD SPEAKS

There are other Biblical ways that God speaks to His people. There are visitations of angels and visitations of Jesus. God can take you to the heavenly realms in the spirit like He did to Paul and John. You could be trans-relocated in your body to other regions on the earth like Phillip and Elijah were. I know these encounters sound so far-fetched and unattainable, but all the individual accounts in the Bible happened to real normal people like you and me. It's good not to mystify Bible characters like Marvel comic superheroes. God is the same today as He was then, and He is no respecter of persons. God does not have Paul, John, Phillip and Elijah to advance His kingdom. He has Julie, Sally, Tom, Randy, you and me. So set your heart on Jesus and all that is possible in Him. Every Bible story and experience is fair game to believe for.

My Son Stephen's Angelic Encounters

At the time of this writing, my oldest son Stephen is 18 years old. He started asking God to open his eyes to the unseen realm when he was around 12 years old. Over the last few years he has had several profound encounters and visitations with angels.

Stephen began asking God to see his guardian angel when he first heard that we are able to train our spiritual senses. He would spend time each night practicing to see his angel. Here is a story in his own words about the first time he saw his angel.

"I was trying to see my angel before I went to bed. I would turn off my lights, so it was dark and I looked into the corner of my room. I was focusing there and all of a sudden I saw a silhouette of a person. I got really, really scared, so I put my face under my covers and said, 'Okay, I'm done. I'm going to bed.' Then I thought, 'Wait, since my angel already rooms with me, maybe I could keep going on with this.' So then with my head still under the covers, I said to my angel, 'You can come sit on my bed if you want.' But I was still scared and hiding under my covers. A couple seconds later I felt my bed impress. I felt something physical sitting on my bed and leaning against my leg. Then my leg started to vibrate and I felt the power of God going into my leg. That was cool!"

A couple years ago Stephen joined me on a ministry trip to Southern California. I had him share a teaching and testimony based on Hebrews 5:14 about how he started to train his spiritual senses to be able see the angelic.

"For those who through constant practice have their spiritual faculties carefully trained to distinguish good from evil" (Hebrew 5:14 Weymouth).

He prayed for the congregation's spiritual eyes to be opened to see. That weekend several people reported having profound open-eye visitations of angels.

During one service we washed the feet of the senior pastor and his wife and prayed over them. A teenage girl was praying for them. Suddenly she screamed and started to tremble and cry. She exclaimed, "I see a giant angel standing behind you two. It's as tall as the ceiling!" Immediately a tangible holy presence and awe filled the room.

That night a group of high school youth went home from our service to a friend's house and started to have a soaking prayer session. They have never tried soaking prayer before, and most of the youth felt water washing over them. One young man felt someone grab his arms and yank them up. He opened his eyes expecting to see one of his friends. He was shocked when his eyes beheld a person that was glowing with pure light. An angel was holding his arms.

These high-schoolers got so filled with the presence of God, they said, "We need to go give this away to someone!" They went to the corner gas station and saw a group of people. One teenager felt a word of knowledge for someone's left wrist that needed healing. They asked the group if anyone needed their left wrist healed. One person said, "Yes." They prayed and God healed the wrist. Then they shared the love of God through the Gospel of Jesus, and some people in that group got saved!

That weekend God's kingdom came in miraculous power. We saw seven deaf ears opened, two wheelchairs emptied, and several tumors dissolved. Many were powerfully touched by the presence and love of God.

 **ACTION STEP**

- Watch Video #5 - Word of Knowledge

Chapter Six

WHO ARE YOU?

"You were born to be amazing." – Kris Vallotton

If you do not know who you are, then you will never truly live to become who you are called to be. Identity theft is one of the most popular crimes in the Church today. Many believers do not truly know who they are. Because of this they are not walking in the fullness of the destiny God has for them. We were all created to change the world, to bring kingdom transformation to our sphere of influence. To do this we must know who we are and whose we are.

Our Father Wants Us

"There aren't any foster kids in heaven." – Dr. Alan Chin, my dad

Recently I visited my dad and stepmom, Annie. They shared the most incredible story of the adoption process of my four younger sisters. My parents had to fight and overcome some incredible obstacles to finally call these girls their own. I truly hope they write a book about their journey of adoption. One story that stands out is when an adoption expert said, "You should not adopt this girl because..." This was during a preliminary interview. My parents were to look over many potential adoption candidates before making any decision. They privately agreed before the meeting that they would not make any final choices on the children without a careful case study of each child. This adoption agent went on and on, explaining a laundry list of very valid reasons why this particular girl should not be considered a top choice for my parents to adopt. "She has this medical problem...She has trouble with this...She has..." Overwhelmed in the moment, my dad slammed his hand down on this girl's adoption file and declared, "No! This is my girl. I want her!"

The decision was made, and I now have a wonderful little sister that is very much amazing and loved by a marvelous, caring family. I truly believe this reflects how our heavenly Father chooses and adopts us. There are many accurate accusers pointing to a endless list of all our shortcomings, shouting to God, "You should not take him because...." God our Father slams his hand down on our age-long file of sins and flaws and emphatically announces, "No! This is my boy. I want him!" "No! This is my girl. I want her!" Our Father deeply loves and wants us!

> *"Having predestined us to adoption as sons by Jesus Christ to Himself, according to the good pleasure of His will"* (Ephesians 1:5).

> *"For you did not receive the spirit of bondage again to fear, but you received the Spirit of adoption by whom we cry out, "Abba, Father"* (Romans 8:15).

Father's Extravagant Love

The foundation of our identity must be entirely solid, true and based on Father God's unconditional love toward us. Our identity must originate and end with who Heavenly Father says we are. Unfortunately many of us have had poor examples of fathering. When this happens it is common to transfer our Heavenly Father's nature to our earthly examples. I personally experienced a very violent and abusive childhood. I grew up to hate two stepfathers in my life. When I got saved I experienced the love of Jesus, but Father God intimidated me. Although I forgave these broken fathers, I still did not feel safe with Father God. I thought He, too, must be unavailable, distant or at least a little mean and mad. In first year BSSM we read the book *The Father's Embrace* by Jack Frost, and I received the personal revelation of an up-close, loving and kind Father. That revealing of His true nature has transformed my identity and my security. We all need a continual revelation and encounter with Father's unconditional love towards us individually.

So what does Father God think about us and what is He truly like?

Father God thinks the world of us. Father declares we have utmost importance and value to Him. Something's value is determined by the price someone is willing to pay for it. Our Father felt we were worth the life of His very own Son while we were still sinners. *"But God demonstrates His own love toward us, in that while we were still sinners, Christ died for us"* (Romans 5:8). Astronomical is the value He places on us!

Let's take a closer look at the Father's extravagant nature in Luke 15. This parable shadows and unveils Father God's incredible love toward us. This is commonly called the parable of the prodigal son. The word prodigal is characterized by profuse or wastefulness, recklessly spendthrift, or to lavish. We often focus on the son's careless nature and call him the prodigal in this story. I would like to point out that this story is more about a Father's love that seems prodigal and unrestrained in nature.

We are familiar with the events of how the younger son completely shipwrecked his life. A modern day insurance adjuster would have called his life a total loss. Luckily for him and us, our Heavenly Father chooses to give us what we do not deserve. In this story the younger son asked for his inheritance that was to be bestowed upon the death of his father. He was basically communicating, "Father, I wish you were dead!" The younger son consumed all of his inheritance on riotous living and headed homeward solely for the sake of a meal. The father saw his son from afar and ran out to meet his boy. In that culture for an elder to run was considered most undignified. Yet uninhibited, he embraced, kissed, forgave and loved his son, even before the son asked for his father's forgiveness.

The story proceeds,

"But the father said to his servants, 'Quick! Bring the best robe and put it on him. Put a ring on his finger and sandals on his feet. Bring the fattened calf and kill it. Let's have a feast and celebrate. For this son of mine was dead and is alive again; he was lost and is found.' So they began to celebrate" (Luke 15:22-24 NIV).

The restorative love and forgiveness were always there. The father did not ask his son to apologize or to even prove himself trustworthy again to earn his father's love. No, the father's love was simply changeless and unrestrained. His lavish love was a constant, abiding and unalterable reality. And so is Father's love toward us. In this story, Jesus allows us a glimpse into the heart and very nature of God. God our Father is prodigal with his unending compassion and love towards us.

"See what great love the Father has lavished on us, that we should be called children of God! And that is what we are!" (1 John 3:1).

Lavished implies that Father's love toward us is overly, abundantly poured out, as if He is recklessly spendthrift and wasteful. I'm sure the Father's love is so extravagant toward us that a tight-fisted accountant could view His investment as foolishly wasteful. His love is constantly and profusely poured out toward us, separate from our performance or shortcomings. Luke 15 is about a prodigal's Father's love toward us his children.

WORKING FROM LOVE, NOT FOR IT

Jesus knew His identity. Father God had immovably ingrained His security, His acceptance and His approval toward His Son. Look at what Father declared at Jesus' baptism.

> *"This is my Son, whom I love; with him I am well pleased"* (Matthew 3:17 NIV).

The Father gave Jesus His security, You are my Son. His acceptance--Whom I love, and His approval-- In Whom I am well pleased right up front. The Father gave Jesus His true identity before He performed any good works or a single miracle was recorded.

Why is that so important to us?

It is imperative that we see the Father's love and acceptance have nothing to do with any good works. It is important for us to know God's love and acceptance do not hinge at all on our Christian performance. He loves us because that is who He is! We can take no credit for that. *"This is love, not that we loved God, but that He loved us and sent His Son to be the propitiation for our sins"* (1 John 4:10). Our identity as loved sons and daughters of Father is the most powerful insight we can get. Our security in sonship is based completely in His great love for us, period!

In our society, it is normal for people to work for love. Sadly many folks today have a fatherless, orphaned heart. An orphaned heart is when we feel like we have to fight for love, acceptance and security. We do things to be accepted and to know who we are. Many people are in career fields not because they are passionate about it, but because there is a social acceptance assigned to that position. They are working in a certain career field to be approved. I am so thankful that it does not work like that in our Father's kingdom. Our Father adopts us and we receive the spirit of adoption at our new birth. We get our identity and acceptance right up front.

From that place of being loved and accepted, we can love others. We are working from love, not for it. What a difference!

Saint vs. Sinner

Here is a tale of a poor individual having an identity crisis. Do you remember the story of the ugly duckling? The mother duck is sitting on a nest of eggs, and one egg is much larger than the rest. When this larger egg hatches, the ugliest duckling she has ever seen is exposed. As the story goes on, all the ducklings ridicule and torment their brother, because he looks and acts so differently from the rest. But wait, an epiphany is about to happen for this peculiar creature. Let's pick up the story from here.

> However, by springtime, he had grown so big that the farmer decided: "I'll set him free by the pond!" That was when the duckling saw himself mirrored in the water. "Goodness! How I've changed! I hardly recognize myself," the duckling exclaimed.
>
> The flight of swans winged north again and glided on to the pond. When the duckling saw them, he realized he was one of their kind, and soon made friends. "We're swans like you!" they said, warmly. "Where have you been hiding?" "It's a long story," replied the young swan, still astounded. Now, he swam majestically with his fellow swans. One day, he heard children on the riverbank exclaim: "Look at that young swan! He's the finest of them all!" And he almost burst with happiness.[1]

When did the ugly duckling become a swan? Was it when he

first viewed his image in the water? No, he was a swan from the moment he was created. Likewise, we are changed the second we are born again in Christ. This swan just didn't know who he really was, so he acted like a duck. He tried to walk and quack like a duck even though the whole time he was a swan. In the same way, it is pivotal for us to realize what happened when we were made anew at our rebirth. Then we will walk right.

I want to expose a common identity theft statement. I hear many Christians confess, "I am just a sinner saved by grace." That statement sounds innocent and humble enough, but there is a real danger lying in wait behind that phrase. If I state that I am just a sinner, then I identify myself as still being a sinner. I have some monumental good news. We used to be sinners, past tense. By the blood of Jesus we are no longer sinners. Now we are saints of God! Halleluiah!

The Bible says I have a complete new nature and that I am now dead to sin. My old man has passed away. My old sin nature is dead, dead, dead. *Likewise you also, reckon yourselves to be dead indeed to sin, but alive to God in Christ Jesus our Lord"* (Romans 6:11). Our identity is no longer in being a sinner (the old man). We now identify ourselves in being a new creation. If I identify myself as still being a sinner, an ugly duckling, then I will never embrace my real nature of a saint, a swan. If I think I am still a sinner saved by grace, I will act like a sinner does and sin. It will actually give me the grace to sin by faith. Let me repeat that. If I confess and identify that I am a sinner saved by grace, it will actually give me the grace to sin by faith. *"As a man thinks in his heart so shall he be"* (Proverbs 23:7).

A NEW CREATION

"Therefore, if anyone is in Christ, he is a new creation; old things have passed away; behold, all things have become new " (2 Corinthians 5:17).

People often get cover-up tattoos to hide the names of their exes. They want to conceal a time in their past, along with the tag-along memories. Their hope is to go forward into a new brighter future. This is understandable. New fresh ink is one of the only choices available to them to show a reformation from their past. This may be helpful in regard to tattoos on our natural body and skin. But it is not so with our soul and our spirit. Jesus did not die on the cross to conceal or cover up our old sinful man. Jesus came to kill it! Jesus destroyed the power of sin and death in the Christian. Our old nature is now dead! The second we are born again we become new creations. Jesus answered, *"I tell you the truth, no one can enter the kingdom of God unless he is born of water and the Spirit"* (John 3:5 NIV). Our first birth is a natural water birth. Our second is of the Spirit. When we became born again the blood of Jesus made us brand new creations. *"Therefore, if anyone is in Christ, he is a new creation; old things have passed away; behold, all things have become new"* (2 Corinthians 5:17).

His blood transfigured us into a new being, a new creation of righteousness. The Greek word used for creation in this verse is ktisis. The definition – "creation (creature) which is founded from nothing." It is the same word used when God created the new heavens and the earth in Genesis chapter one. We are this kind of brand-new in Christ. We may appear the same looking into the mirror, but, oh boy, have we been changed! 2 Corinthians 5:21

states, *"For He made Him who knew no sin to be sin for us, that we might become the righteousness of God in Him."* This verse says we are now the righteousness of God in Christ Jesus. That is incredible! We are the righteousness of God in Christ. Say who you are out loud, "I am the righteousness of God in Christ Jesus." Let that sink in. You are not a sinner. You are a new creation saint, and the righteousness of God in Christ Jesus.

But why do I still mess up at times and sin if I am really completely new?

> *"Therefore do not let sin reign in your mortal bodies that you should obey it in its lusts. And do not present your members as instruments of unrighteousness to sin, but present yourselves to God as being alive from the dead, and your members as instruments of righteousness to God. For sin shall not have dominion over you, for you are not under law but under grace"* (Rom. 6:12-14).

Because of the cross we have the power to make a choice now. We can live by our new nature and the righteousness of God. Or we can go back to the old nature and empower the nature of sin to manifest in our lives again. Bill Johnson says, "Many believers are using their resurrection power to resurrect the old man." That's where many of the problems come in for believers. Because of the wrong attitudes, or mindsets, that may still remain in the souls of believers, many think that they are still in bondage to sin even though they are not. It is still possible to sin because our souls and our mindsets need to be renewed. But as we grow in maturity with Jesus, this renewing of the mind will occur. Our life outwardly is constantly changing in speech and in action to be more Christ-like.

Jesus' blood took care of sin in the believer's life forever, once and for all. *"By one sacrifice he has made perfect forever those who are being made holy"* (Hebrews 10:14 NIV). God sees us as holy and in right standing before Him only because of the blood of Jesus. If we mess up and sin, we know that is not our true nature and identity anymore. We quickly repent, run back to Father's love and His complete forgiveness. We look into the loving eyes of Jesus and declare, "Self, you are the righteousness of God in Christ Jesus!"

Look at how Paul addressed the believers as saints in his letters to the churches. He did not write, "To the sinners at Ephesus" or "To the backslidden at Colossae." Although Paul did address certain sin issues at these churches, he still entitled them saints. "To the saints in Ephesus..." he wrote. He was calling them up to their true nature and their rightly placed identity. Paul was saying, "Hey guys, maybe you forgot who you are, but you are saints and a royal priesthood."

It is imperative to have a Jesus consciousness rather that sin consciousness. Proverbs 23:7 shows us that what we think upon in our heart will bear fruit in our lives. If we continually focus our attention on trying not to sin, that sin will actually be empowered to increase in our life. What we focus on will increase. If I am insistently thinking, "I need to quit smoking. I need to quit smoking. Man, I really need to quit smoking!" What am I continually putting before my thoughts? You got it, smoking. Having smoking in my mind continually will empower the desire to want to smoke. Likewise, if we fix our thoughts on Jesus and how forgiven and righteous we are, that will increase in our life, and sin will lose its hold. The power of Jesus and His forgiveness will increase as we focus on that. As we put our attention and affection on Jesus, sin issues will by nature fall off our lives. Ultimately Jesus is the perfecter of our faith, not our good deeds. *"Let us fix our eyes on Jesus, the author and perfecter of our faith"* (Hebrew 12:2 NIV). Be intentional about centering your gaze on Jesus, His great love and His complete forgiveness for you.

> *"But you are a chosen people, a royal priesthood, a holy nation, a people belonging to God, that you may declare the praises of him who called you out of darkness into his wonderful light"* (1 Peter 2:9 NIV).

BEING THE BELOVED

In Chicago last year the Lord spoke to me. He said, "I am going to give you a deeper revelation of my love for you, which will change how you love others." He gave me this Scripture: *"We love because He first loved us"* (1 John 4:19). The ability to love others is in direct proportion to our ability to receive unconditional love from Him. The more we receive His love, the more capable we are to give love away. God told me that I needed to enlarge how I view His love toward me like John the beloved did. He said one of John's greatest strengths was that he realized that he was the disciple that Jesus loved. No one else wrote that John was the one Jesus loved, only John did. It was a personal epiphany that John had.

God showed me that it is so much more important to boast in His love toward me, rather than my love for Him. Let me show you the difference. Remember at the Last Supper when Peter boasted in his love toward Jesus saying, "Even if all these desert you, I will not! I will die before I deny you." Peter was boasting in his love toward

God. Remember how well that worked out for Peter. We all know that Peter denied Jesus three times to a servant girl. John, on the other hand, was resting on Jesus' bosom, representing his trust in Jesus' love toward him. John was resting in God's love toward him. He was boasting in God's love toward him. John was trusting in the revelation of being God's beloved.

Let me show you why this is so important. Who was the only disciple standing at the foot of the cross? The Bible records that only John was there. Why? Because John had his trust in God's perfect unfailing love toward him, not in his own imperfect love toward God. John was securely rooted and grounded in God's inexhaustible love toward him. That gave John concrete safety and security.

THE FULLNESS OF GOD

> *"That Christ may dwell in your hearts through faith; that you, being rooted and grounded in love, may be able to comprehend with all the saints (not sinners) what the width and length and depth and height— to know the love of Christ which passes knowledge; that you may be filled with all the fullness of God"* (Ephesians 3:17-19).

Paul is equating the fullness of God as a revelation of Christ's love toward us. Could it be that the fullness of God, the mysteries of the kingdom, lies in a deeper revelation of the love of Christ? The fullness of God awaits in a greater epiphany of being His beloved. I believe we have just scratched the surface of the revelation of His love toward us.

Remember at Jesus' baptism, the Father said, "This is my beloved

Son..." But notice when Satan tempted Jesus in the wilderness, he left off the beloved part saying, "If you are the Son of God..." He intentionally did not say, "If you are the beloved Son of God." The devil knows when we realize we are the beloved of God, we become extremely dangerous and risky. We start to believe the most ridiculous and impossible dreams of "If God is for us, who could be against us!" When a child feels loved, safe and secure in their father's love and His presence, they become quite bold and fearless. When we really understand that we are the beloved of God, no assault against our identity will prevail. The attack is against being the beloved of God.

David knew he was loved of God. His name literally meant "the beloved." Every time his father called him David, he was reminded that he was loved. It is no coincidence that this revelation of being loved of God gave him the courage to face the lion, the bear and eventually Goliath to save all of Israel. The revelation of being God's beloved will give us courage to take great risks, to love others and to do great exploits with Him. The Bible says, "Perfect love casts out fear." Perfect love is God's love, not ours. It is the revelation of God's love toward us that will make us bold as a lion.

Magnify His Love Towards You

Do you know that God really loves you? Most people understand that God loves them in a general sense. God loves everybody, right? Yes, He does. But let me show you why we must magnify His love toward us personally. Let's say the blades of grass in your front yard represent a multitude of people and the sunlight is God's broad love toward mankind. What would happen if you took a magnifying glass and focused that love (sunlight) on one single blade of grass?

It would heat up and eventually light on fire. That is exactly what happens when we focus on God's love toward us individually. It heats up our heart and sets us on fire. We become fearless in love.

There was a season when every time I started to say, "Jesus, I love you," the Holy Spirit stopped me and told me to say, "Jesus, You love me." He said, "I want you to recognize My love for you at least twice as much as you recognize your love toward Me." I started practicing magnifying His love toward me. When we sing songs that say, "Jesus, you love us," I now change that to "Jesus, you love me." I am practicing a revelation of His love toward me. I love because He first loved me.

When I worked at Olive Garden, I would say to myself repeatedly, "I am the Olive Garden server whom Jesus loves." This awareness of His love toward me has caused a supernatural favor to surround me wherever I go. What we give attention to and focus on will grow and bear fruit in our lives. While serving one day, I made a mistake and rang in a food order incorrectly. When the entrees came to the table, I noticed the wrong entree I had ordered on my tray. When I went back to the kitchen to have them make the correct dish, just by chance the correct entree I needed was already cooked and ready in the window. They said they "accidentally" had made an extra one! I quickly brought the right entree to the table. It appeared as if I had never made a mistake at all. Everyone was happy, especially me! God has been teaching me how the revelation and recognition of being His beloved surrounds me with His goodness and favor. It is getting harder for me to make mistakes now that stick when I focus on my identity as the beloved of God. He seems to have my mess-ups blanketed even before I make them.

A revelation of a truth will always change the facts. You are the beloved of God!

BEING YOURSELF

"One of the greatest sins you can commit as a believer is comparing yourself to someone else" - Jason Vallotton

We are about to start training in the gifts of the Spirit, so that we may release God's kingdom to those around us. Before we do, I want to talk to you about you getting to be you, apart from any comparison with others. When the Holy Spirit showed up in Acts 2, the Bible says, *"When the day of Pentecost came, they were all together in one place. Suddenly a sound like the blowing of a violent wind came from heaven and filled the whole house where they were sitting. They saw what seemed to be tongues of fire that separated and came to rest on each of them. All of them were filled with the Holy Spirit"* (Acts 2 1-4 NIV). It says that the tongues of fire separated and came to rest on each person. It was a corporate encounter, yet very personal at the same time. It wasn't a blanket or wave of fire that hit the crowd. The fire separated and rested individually on unique persons.

When I asked the Holy Spirit why He came in that way, He said to me, "I anoint individuals and reveal myself to each personality separately." He was showing me how He really values the uniqueness in every person. You are not like any other person that has ever lived or will live on this planet. You are one-of-a-kind on purpose! There is only one you and the Holy Spirit on your life is specific and special. You and He make a special flavor of anointing that this world desperately needs. Everyone has his or her own flavor, but you need to stay true to who you are, so the world gets a chance to see Jesus in you. There is a unique expression of God's nature that can only be released through your life as you are poured out in love.

When we try to be like someone else, we lose our freedom and put shackles on ourselves. *"It is for freedom that Christ has set us free. Stand firm, then, and do not let yourselves be burdened again by a yoke of slavery"* (Galatians 5:1 NIV). This passage is not only talking about us being free from sin. Jesus came for freedom's sake so we can be free to really be us!

In a supernatural culture of miracles, it is easy to start comparing yourself with others that appear more anointed and gifted than you. When prophesying, some will get very specific details into people's lives like names and birthdays. Others will share radical healing testimonies. Unless your identity is based on who you are and not in what you do, it could be easy to fall into revival performance. A voice starts telling you, "I have to heal somebody today to feel good about myself. Or I have to keep up with Johnny and Missy. They are getting everybody saved, healed and delivered. I need a testimony to share this week to feel loved and accepted." Pretty soon we are doing exactly what the world does for love and acceptance, but it is in context of a revival culture. It appears sacred and righteous on the outside, but, if left unchecked, it will fester and breed identity treachery for us.

Any time we are doing things for love and not from love we are headed for trouble, leading straight into an identity crisis. Somewhere in us, a lie against our true identity has sucker punched us. When I start noticing that I am trying to work for love and not from it, I ask the Holy Spirit, "Holy Spirit, why am I not feeling power-ful and free to be me right now? Is there a lie that I am believing?" If He shows me a lie, I pray a prayer to break the power of that lie, and then I ask the Holy Spirit what the truth is. I then take a moment and absorb the truth of what the Holy Spirit brought to me. *"Then you will know the truth, and the truth will set you free"* (John 8:32 NIV).

INTIMACY AND IDENTITY

"When you forget who you are and whose you are,
you start to compromise." - Kris Vallotton

The two greatest strengths in a believer's life are their intimacy with God and their identity in God. Satan is not trying to get you to sin. He is attacking your intimacy with God and trying to ambush your identity in Him. If he can get you to lose your intimacy and to forget who you are, then sin is a natural by-product. Intimacy and identity are top-most priorities for our spiritual well-being.

If you forget who you are, just fall into Father's unconditional extravagant love toward you. Say to yourself, "My identity is that I am a loved son or daughter of God apart from any performance. I am truly the beloved of God." Then look into His smiling eyes of approval and His unmerited acceptance, and rest in your identity in Him. You are loved one hundred percent!

ENDNOTES

1. The Ugly Duckling is a literary fairy tale by Danish poet and author Hans Christian Andersen (1805 – 1875).

ACTION STEP

- Watch Video #6 - Father's Love Letter

Chapter 7

Heaven Invading Earth

"Your kingdom come. Your will be done on earth as it is in heaven." - Jesus Christ

As I was growing up, we recited the Lord's Prayer in our school every morning. At that time, I had no idea what I was declaring each day. Do you know that unless you have a revelation of a truth, the words of that truth are powerless to you? I did not have any revelation of the Lord's Prayer I recited; therefore I had no fruit in my life to show for all those words that I uselessly declared so many times. This is why it is essential that we not only read the Scriptures, but that we get a personal epiphany of what the Scriptures mean. An epiphany is a sudden understanding of the meaning of something. It is a personal revelation.

I want to focus our attention on one verse in the Lord's Prayer that speaks about the kingdom of God. Let's take a closer look at this verse to discover what Jesus was trying to communicate to us. Jesus was giving us insight into three distinct truths.

Jesus told us to pray to the Father, *"Your kingdom come, your will be done on earth as it is in heaven"* (Matthew 6:10).

1.   Jesus is expressing that the earth currently does not look like it does in heaven.

2.   It is God's will and His desire that the earth would look like the kingdom of heaven.

3.   It is possible for earth to look like the kingdom of heaven since Jesus tells us to pray for that.

To sum it up, Jesus is saying it is God's will for us to bring His kingdom to earth now, so earth can start to look like heaven. Let's take a look at what a kingdom is. A kingdom speaks of a king's domain. It has various implications, but a simple way to explain it is to think about what a king or monarch symbolizes. A king is set up to have absolute rule and reign over a specific region. There are special governmental laws and regulations that rule in that region. Other kingdoms may have different laws that their citizens have to abide by. However, in each region, the people are legally bound to obey their king's rules and regulations.

There is a story of a U.S. Naval officer that went to Great Britain on vacation. He was leaving a local tavern in his rented Aston Martin V12. He pulled out onto the street. Crash! Out of nowhere, an oncoming farm tractor smashed right into the front of his rental auto, crumpling the car's luxurious hood. The irate and semi-intoxicated officer jumped out of his car and started yelling at the farmer. The British farmer said, "You think you are in the right because you are on the right side of the road, but there is a big problem. You're in the United Kingdom now, and here we drive on the left side of the road. I hope you have good auto insurance!" The officer had pulled out onto the right side of the road forgetting that he was NOT in the United States anymore. He was no longer in his home kingdom. What was right in the United States was very wrong in Great Britain. Likewise God has set up His spiritual kingdom with laws to govern spiritual matters. God's kingdom rule and His reign are designed to trump all lesser spiritual kingdoms.

Question: What weighs up to 910,000 pounds (equivalent to a small train), and can fly?

Answer: The Boeing 747-400ER Freighter aircraft.

This enormous airplane is able to fly, because the law of lift over this airplane's wings overpowers the opposing law of gravity. Both laws remain in effect during flight. The law of gravity never departs during flight but a dominant law of lift overruns the forces of gravity when enough force or speed is applied. That's similar to how God's kingdom is able to overpower lesser kingdoms. The kingdom of God has NO limits. Kingdoms of darkness are able to be defeated and natural physical laws can be subdued with God's unlimited kingdom power.

Our mandate is to carry our Father's heavenly kingdom and His governing rule into our surroundings--earth. It is heaven's kingdom invading earth, until earth starts reflecting God's ways and attributes. We are authorized to restore things to their original intended purpose and design. When Adam and Eve sinned, God's original plan got shipwrecked. When Jesus came, He defeated the devil and gave us back the keys to the kingdom, restoring earth and mankind to God's original plan. It is a ministry of reconciliation. The kingdom of God inherently gravitates toward invading and changing the seemingly impossible. Jesus could walk on water because God's kingdom and rule are above earth's natural laws. Jesus multiplied a few fish to feed the multitudes. God's kingdom invaded and supplied a need.

Do you realize what happens when someone's broken foot is instantly healed or a tumor dissolves during prayer? It is God's heavenly kingdom--His government and domain--invading. When a couple gets saved and their marriage is restored, God's governmental laws of life and love just showed up to occupy. What about when a suicidal spirit is driven from a young person's life? The kingdom of God is present. *"But if I cast out demons with the finger of God, surely the kingdom of God has come upon you"* (Luke 11:20). We are God's good-news soldiers called to liberate those around us.

Two Opposing Kingdoms

My destiny is to go to heaven; my responsibility is to bring heaven." – Bill Johnson

There are two opposing kingdoms at work on the earth. There is the kingdom of light and the kingdom of darkness, God's kingdom and Satan's. Each of these spiritual kingdoms affects the natural realm in which we live. One kingdom brings death, the other life.

SUE'S HAUNTED HOUSE

I originally met Sue at Safeway holding a sign saying, "Please help me bury me brother." I asked Sue if we could pray that her brother be raised from the dead. Jesus is still into dead raising. I gave Sue our phone number and a week later she phoned me very distraught. She said she had heard her brother's voice in her head at her brother's cremation service, and he was very angry. At that moment she felt something enter her stomach. She said it started to move in her stomach, and it caused so much pain she quickly left to the restroom. Sue was in so much abdominal pain she had to have someone else drive her home.

That night at home all hell broke loose. Her daughters started to scream, saying something was biting and scratching them. Some unseen force was leaving scratches and bite marks on their bodies. Sue called me frantically the next morning and asked if we could help her family out. I prayed for Sue over the phone, and the phone call dropped. When I called back, Sue said all the power went off in their house and the microwave was flashing 666. I got really excited. I like having confrontations with the demonic, because it usually means Jesus is about to set someone free into His liberty with His love.

When we arrived at Sue's house, she was in bed. As we started to pray, Sue's eyes started to flutter and they rolled back into her head. She started to laugh and snarl in a demonic voice. We are

---

neither afraid nor impressed with the demonic, because Jesus only is King. We commanded that we talk to Sue and not the demon. For about thirty minutes Sue came in and out of consciousness, struggling with the demonic. She was able to forgive her mom and brother for committing the most heinous crimes against her as a little girl. It was heart breaking and horrific hearing the satanic ritualistic abuse she endured as a young child.

When Sue chose to forgive her mother and brother, the demonic condition lifted and great peace filled the house. Right away Sue's sister ran inside the room saying, "I heard thunder and I saw a black smoke cloud come out of the wall and leave your room." Jesus set Sue free through the power of forgiveness! The family turned their hearts and trust to Jesus Christ. Her husband walked outside and turned on the BBQ grill. They started burning all the occultist objects they had in their house on that BBQ. Jesus is victorious; His kingdom is triumphant!

JESUS, THE LIFE GIVER

The Bible is very clear on who is behind all the killing, stealing and destroying. *"The thief (devil) comes only to steal and kill and destroy..."* (John 10:10). What is the intention of sickness and disease? What would sickness and disease do to your body if your immune system was completely shut off and you had no medical and spiritual help? Any sickness, even a common cold, would eventually kill you. Yes, it would kill you dead, dead, dead. Are you seeing my point? The devil comes to kill, steal and destroy. Now let's look at the mission of Jesus.

"...I (Jesus) have come that they may have life, and have it to the full" (John 10:10 NIV).

"The reason the Son of God appeared was to destroy the devil's work" (1 John 3:8 NIV).

"How God anointed Jesus of Nazareth with the Holy Spirit and with power, who went about doing good and healing all who were oppressed by the devil, for God was with Him" (Acts 10:38).

"And as you go, preach, saying, 'The kingdom of heaven is at hand.' Heal the sick, cleanse the lepers, raise the dead, cast out demons. Freely you have received, freely give." (Matthew 10:7-8).

GOD PARTNERS

How is God planning to advance His kingdom on earth? Through you and me. God's will and mission will be accomplished through His people. He chooses us to be His change agents and world changers. Let's look at the story of God and Moses that illustrates this principle from the burning bush in Exodus, Chapter 3:

"The Lord said, "I have indeed seen the misery of my people in Egypt. I have heard them crying out because of their slave drivers, and I am concerned about their suffering. So I have come down to rescue them...." I imagine at this point Moses was cheering God on, "Cool! Way to go, God! I'm glad You are going to do something about their hardships. That's awfully nice of You." Moses heard

God say what God was going to do. Nonetheless, in His very next breath, listen to what God says to Moses, *"So now, go. I am sending you!"* Moses must have turned his head sideways with a confused look, "What? Hold on! Wait a minute, God. You just said you were coming down and you were going to rescue them! What do you mean that You are sending me? You don't need me. You are God." God confidently replies, "I am going to rescue them just like I said, but it will be done through you, so now go." God chooses to fulfill His plans through his kids.

It's intriguing to see how Moses reacts similarly to Gideon to the call of God. Moses' first words after God gave him the mission is, *"Who am I, that I should go?"* (Exodus 3:11). Moses felt under-anointed and under-qualified. It appears that God's standard of qualification is not great degrees or pedigrees, but vessels willing to trust and go. *"But God has chosen the foolish things of the world to put to shame the wise, and God has chosen the weak things of the world to put to shame the things which are mighty"* (1 Corinthians 1:27). God is searching the world for willing lovers that will say, "Yes!" He can make these followers that may seem foolish into dreaded champions for Him.

Like Gideon and Moses, God is calling you to do something great. Most likely we will feel unsure and unprepared for what God asks us to do. That's okay. God only asks that we say "yes," trust and follow Him. The Holy Spirit is called the Comforter for a reason. We will need comfort for what God asks us to do. We will, in all likelihood, never feel secure in what God is asking us to do, because He asks us to do the impossible. We can only be secure in knowing who God is. He sends us into impossible situations to be the answer.

126

Our trust is secure in the fact that He goes with us.

TOUCHING THE UNCLEAN

In the Old Testament if you touched a leper you were made unclean according to Jewish law. The leper's sin polluted you and you became contaminated. When Jesus showed up with the kingdom of God, everything changed. Now when the leper touched Jesus, Jesus did not become unclean but the leper was made whole. The kingdom of God over-turned the kingdom of sin and sickness. God's Kingdom overpowered evil with good; life overcame death.

NIGHT AT THE CASINO

The Lord enlightened me about His kingdom rule one night at our local Indian casino. I want to introduce you to Reggie. Reggie is a father in his late twenties and drives a shuttle bus for the casino. When Reggie picked us up, he smiled and said with a wink, "There are a lot of pretty girls here tonight, if you know what I mean." We also smiled and replied, "My friend, we are actually here for a different reason than girls tonight." We asked Reggie if he knew that his left leg was shorter than his right one. He said, "Yes it is. Why would you ask?" We told him we would like to fix that for him. We prayed for his leg to lengthen and for his bad knees too. Reggie said he was on light duty because of his painful knee condition. He told us he would check his knees out to see if he was healed during his lunch break. We went inside and started ministering to people as they gambled. We saw many miracles and healing inside the casino. Backs, hips and knees were healed. After a couple of hours of releasing

---

miracles in the casino, I went to find Reggie. I asked a security guard if he knew where Reggie was. He said, "Reggie left, but before he left I saw him running laps around the parking lot."

We went back to the Indian casino a couple weeks later and Reggie found us. Excitedly he said, "Can I talk to you a minute in private?" We stepped outside and what he said next paradigm-shifted the way I view the kingdom of God. Reggie continued, "Remember the night you guys prayed for me? Well, I ran around the parking lot and my leg and knees were completely healed. But there is more. My daughter had a life threatening disease when she was younger and we have had a massive doctor bill that we have been trying to settle in the courts for years. We just got a letter saying the hospital decided to release us from that huge debt and that we don't owe them a single penny! And there is even more! It's like our entire family has been changed completely from the moment I met you guys. I can't put my finger on it, but everything has changed. We started going to church and everything."

Through Reggie's story, God showed me that when we pray for physical healing, there is so much more that happens in the realm of the spirit. Jesus and His disciples proclaimed, *"The kingdom of heaven is at hand"* (Mathew 10:7). When we pray for people, the kingdom is released into their lives. The kingdom is far greater and includes more than a healing or single miracle. It is health and life imparted to all areas of life. It is restoration of marriages, increase of finances, and relationships being made whole. The high places are brought low and the crooked places are made straight. Everything in heaven now becomes available to them.

A person gets an impartation of the kingdom of God when we pray for their headache or a bad knee. The kingdom is not compartmentalized where you just get the miracle part. Whether they like it or not, they get a dose of the entire kingdom in a capsule. Sometimes, it may be released over time, but they just got injected with far more goodness than a physical healing! That's some really good news! Whether I see them healed or not in that moment, I have confidence that the kingdom of God was released into their lives for their good.

 **ACTION STEP**

- Watch Video # 7 - A Life Changed

Chapter 8

MOVING IN POWER

"The gospel without power is not good news." – Bill Johnson

In 2011 I had a dream that I was in a house sitting on a bed in another room while some Christian leaders were talking amongst themselves in the living room. I was eavesdropping on their conversation. One leader said, "We, as a church, used to heal the sick but as we grew, it became too controversial for us, so we stopped." Another leader said, "Yes, we do not pray for the sick anymore either. It was too messy and cost us too much. It was better for us to keep it safe." Something broke loose deep inside of me, and I ran into the living room weeping and pleading with these leaders, "The gospel has to be proven in power. It has to be demonstrated. It must be!"

I woke up crying, still declaring, "The gospel has to be proven in power. It has to be demonstrated. It must be!" I was greatly moved in my spirit. My heart was grieving; I felt like I had lost a loved one. I felt that God was allowing me to feel His heart about the importance of moving in His power. *"For the kingdom of God is not a matter of talk but of power"* (1 Corinthians 4:20 NIV). God was speaking to me how it grieves the Holy Spirit when we don't allow Him to prove the gospel of Jesus in power to those around us. Jesus paid an enormous price so that people could be set free.

> *"He was wounded for our transgressions, He was bruised for our iniquities; the chastisement for our peace was upon Him, and by His stripes we are healed" (Isaiah 53:5).*

If you haven't watched *The Passion of the Christ* by Mel Gibson, please do so. It is so painful to watch our King and Lord being brutally beaten and tortured. I can hardly stand to watch it, even after the filmmakers decreased the gore of what actually happened. I watched through my fingers and sobbed as Jesus was being tortured at the whipping post. The Holy Spirit started to whisper to my heart with every lash, "That was for cancer…That was for mental disorders…That was for divorce…That was for AIDS…" Jesus paid the horrific price for sin, sickness and disease for the entire world in His body. When we witness God's kingdom invading earth through a miracle or healing, we are seeing Jesus get back what He already purchased through His horrendous pain. He bore all the sickness of the world in his body once and for all so that no one else has to.

FULLY PREACH THE GOSPEL

Power demonstrations of the gospel are so important to fully represent God. Paul even said that the gospel was not fully preached unless power was shown. *"In mighty signs and wonders, by the power of the Spirit of God, so that from Jerusalem and round about to Illyricum I have fully preached the gospel of Christ"* (Romans 15:19). Paul says that mighty accompanying signs and wonders by the power of the Spirit equals the gospel being fully preached. If there is only teaching or only words declaring the kingdom of God without a demonstration, then Paul is saying the good news is only partially being preached. It is not complete without "show and tell."

> *"And my speech and my preaching were not with persuasive words of human wisdom, but in demonstration of the Spirit and of power, that your faith should not be in the wisdom of men but in the power of God."* (1 Corinthians 2:4-5).

Recently we did a youth meeting over Skype and many miracles happened. Many youth came up front to be saved and filled with the Holy Spirit. Power was demonstrated and hearts were captured by King Jesus. The power of God fell on these youth. Many said they would never forget tonight. Why? Because they had heard and seen Jesus in action. The world will not be won without power and love demonstrations. We cannot have one without the other. We must move in power and love just like Jesus modeled. We owe the world an encounter with a God that changes impossible situations. The world is waiting for us to demonstrate His kingdom in power. Jesus modeled a perfect supernatural lifestyle.

I love what Pastor Bill Johnson told us on our first day at BSSM. He said that young fresh graduates from college approach him saying, "I don't know what I'm supposed to do now. I don't know God's will for my life. Should I be a school teacher or a missionary?" Bill will clearly tell them, "Just pick one, and then heal the sick, cast out devils, cleanse the lepers and raise the dead!" Another person will ask him, "I don't know where I'm supposed to live. Should I go back home or move to Africa?" His response is, "Just pick one, and then heal the sick, cast out devils, cleanse the leper and raise the dead!" Sure, we are supposed to seek God's direction for our lives, but Bill Johnson clearly points out that no matter where we go or what we end up doing, God's commission and mandate for our life will always be the same…setting people free!

My friend Sarah met Jane, a mother that was paralyzed from the waist down, confined to a wheelchair for over two years. Jane had been in a car wreck that had severed her spine and had caused total paralysis in her legs. The doctors couldn't help her anymore. They did all they could do. Her husband had to pick up his wife every time she wanted to move from her chair to her bed. Sarah crossed paths with Jane, her husband and her daughter downtown on a Redding street corner. Sarah prayed for Jane's legs. After she prayed the first time, Jane said she felt tingling on her legs. They prayed again and Sarah said, "God is doing something. Let's help you stand up." They picked her up and Jane's legs started to gain strength, and she started to have feeling in them. Her husband

and Sarah started taking some steps with her as they held her up. After a few minutes, she got more strength in her legs and started walking on her own! Jane's daughter said, "Mommy, look. You're walking again!" Jane started to walk faster, and then started to jog around, healed by the power and love of Jesus! Jane and her family adamantly kicked the wheelchair to the side of the curb and left it there. They drove off without the wheelchair saying, "We don't need that thing anymore!"

We owe the world a God encounter!

So buckle up! We are going to start training and activating you in the supernatural. We are going to help get you started in basic prophecy, words of knowledge and healing the sick.

Basic Prophecy

"And it shall come to pass afterward that I will pour out my Spirit on all flesh; Your sons and your daughters shall prophesy, your old men shall dream dreams, your young men shall see visions" (Joel 2:28).

More good news--If you are a believer, then you, too, can prophesy. *"For you can all prophesy one by one, that all may learn, and all may be encouraged"* (1 Corinthians 14:31). I am going to teach you the basics of prophecy. Prophecy is hearing God's voice for an individual person or a people group. It is forth-telling or foretelling in nature. Foretelling is telling specific details about the future.

"When the Spirit of truth comes, he will guide you into all truth. He will not speak on his own but will

tell you what he has heard. He will tell you about the
future" (John 16:13 NLT).

Forth-telling is a prophetic word that causes something to go
forth to be created by God. It is the creative, spoken word of God
where something is created that wasn't there before the word was
spoken.

> *"The earth was without form, and void; and dark-*
> *ness was on the face of the deep. And the Spirit of*
> *God was hovering over the face of the waters. Then*
> *God said, 'Let there be light'; and there was light."*
> (Genesis 1:2-3)

Notice that the Spirit was hovering and then God spoke. His
words created light where there was only darkness. Prophecy is used
to speak and create God's light into the darkness. Everything can
change in an instant after a prophetic word from the Lord is spoken.

Last summer I was talking to Jim, an owner of a brick-laying
company. He was telling me how he had not had a single contract
in over two years, and he had downsized his company to only him.
It did not look good for him because the housing market was in
such a deep slump. I caught myself saying these words to him, "God
is going to bring you business. In fact, He is going to bring you so
much business that your phone will start ringing off the hook. You
will have to turn down jobs because of the abundance of work." As I
was speaking these words to him, my mind was saying, "Jason, are
you out of your mind? We are in a housing recession right now."
The truth was in that moment of prophecy I stepped out of my
mind and into God's.

Two weeks later, a friend of his came up to me with excitement and said, "Did you hear what happened to Jim?" I said, "No, what has happened to him?" She went on, "Jim got a call from a large company that he bid a large job on years ago. They told him they had decided to take his bid, not because he had the lowest bid, but because they liked him the best. Jim said that contract will keep him busy for over two years with a crew. Jim said that the phone has been ringing and ringing, and he has had to turn jobs away." I thought, "Wow, there is real power in the spoken prophetic word of God!"

Most of the time when I prophesy, it is to bring comfort and to encourage people. God gives me good things to say to them, and He tells me what He loves about them. *"But everyone who prophesies speaks to men for their strengthening, encouragement and comfort"* (1 Corinthians 14:3 NIV). Say this out loud, "Prophecy is to strengthen, encourage and comfort people. It is to build them up."

FINDING THE GOLD

At BSSM we are taught that prophecy is pulling out the gold in people's lives. We are God's gold miners, finding the gold in other lives. Anyone can find dirt and rocks, but it is the gold that is precious. It doesn't take a prophet to find dirt (sin) in people's lives. Anyone can see that, but it takes God's heart to speak to people about what He loves about them. Every human being on the planet has a divine purpose and destiny in God. The specific greatness inside of them needs to be brought to the surface. Just like in gold panning, we bring the gold (their God-given greatness) to the surface so they can see it. People are generally very aware of their shortcomings and areas of weakness and sin. Those things are already weighing them down. What they don't know is that

Jesus loves them and He has created them with unique and special qualities. They were born for something incredible in their lifetime. There is gold inside of them, even if they aren't living in their God-given destiny yet. We are called to speak light into the darkness. We are not called to say, "I see darkness." They already know about all the darkness. We are commissioned to create life and light with our words where there is darkness and death.

"See how wonderfully kind, tolerant, and patient God is with you...Can't you see that his kindness is intended to turn you from your sin?" (Romans 2:4 NLT).

Not all encouraging words are prophetic, but all New Testament prophetic words are to be encouraging, strengthening and comforting. Kris Vallotton puts it this way, "If our words are red and God's are blue, we speak our red words, and then God will anoint our words with His blue anointing." Our red words, when anointed with God's blue, will turn to purple. As you begin to step out to love and encourage others around you, God will anoint your words as you move in love. Your words will turn purple, anointed with his power to change lives! With practice you will begin to sense when God's blue gets on your red, and BAM! Life is created through your spoken words. Let's talk about the three parts to basic prophecy.

THREE PARTS TO PROPHECY

1. REVELATION

The first part of prophecy is getting revelation. We talked about some ways to get revelation in Chapter 5, such as visions, impressions, feelings, etc. It is a supernatural piece of information. Most of the time, the revelation will be symbolic in nature and will require unlocking a riddle, allegory or analogy of some sort.

2. Interpretation

The second part is interpreting the revelation that you have received. It is trying to figure out what God wants to say through the revelation that He gave you. It is asking Him why He showed you a specific picture or brought a memory to your mind. You can ask the Holy Spirit what it is about this revelation that He is showing you.

3. Delivery

This step determines if and how you are to give the word. You can ask the Holy Spirit if you should tell the person what you saw. Sometimes, God will show us that we are not supposed to deliver the prophetic word, but instead pray into it, especially if you see sin or darkness. God may just want you to speak the opposite into being. For example, if you saw that someone was struggling with gambling, you may be led to declare, "I believe I see a grace on you to steward wealth." Those words, if from God, will have the grace on them to fulfill that word into their life.

Test the word on yourself before you give it. Did it make you feel strengthened, encouraged and comforted? Did it make you smile inside? That's a good way to gauge if your word is encouraging and passes the test.

I Think, I Feel, Does That Make Sense to You?

Since we are learning to prophecy, it is important to use words in our delivery like, "I think," "I feel," and "Does that make sense to you?" Here is an example, "I feel that you are really good with children, and I think you may have a passion for teaching. Does that make sense to you?" If we deliver it this way, it shows that we are still learning and gives grace if we are off. If we got the word right and she does indeed love kids and is going to school to be a teacher, it would be received with the same power as if you said, "Thus sayeth the Lord." What if you said it this way, "The Lord says you are good with children. God says you should be a school teacher, amen." It would be fine if you were right, but what if you were off?

What if she felt called to work as a nurse in a retirement center? Those words could create damage and confusion in her heart. She might think, "Maybe I am going against God's will with the direction of my life?" What if she followed your word as a career path because she wanted to follow God's lead and you were off? See how important it is to use wisdom and safety in the prophetic. Using "I think," "I feel," and "Does that make sense to you?" creates a safety net in the prophetic.

Another caution is not to give specific directional words such as dates, mates and babies. We are learning to prophesy and do not want to give words that give life-changing direction. If we see the nation of Africa over someone, it is good to say, "I feel like I see Africa over you. Does that make any sense?" If you are right and they have a heart for Africa, this will be a powerful confirmation for them. Do not say, "I see you quitting your job and moving to Africa soon." That may be a partially correct word, but timing is very important in the prophetic. They may be called to Africa, but we don't want that person to move to Africa ten years before God's provision.

While learning basic prophecy please do not prophesy couples, mates and marriages-to-be. Stay clear from prophesying about babies too. These are safe guidelines we are taught at Bethel School of Supernatural Ministry while we learn to hear God's voice at a basic level of the prophetic. These guidelines are set in place to protect others and us while growing in prophecy.

TISSUE BOX

Many times the Lord will give you a single piece of supernatural revelation. When you share that piece, another piece of revelation comes. Then when you share that part, more comes. It is like pulling tissue from a tissue box. You cannot see all the pieces of tissue in the box until you share the one that you can see. God will usually not give you the entire prophetic word that he has for someone up front. He will give you a little part and as you are faithful to share that piece, more will come.

PRIMING THE PROPHETIC PUMP

Here are some simple prophetic activities. If I want to give someone a prophetic word, and I don't feel like I have anything, I will use simple categories to prime my supernatural prophesy pump. I will ask God things like, "What animal does this person remind me of?" When I think of a specific animal, I think of all the attributes that make this animal special. Then I assume that person also possesses similar traits since that is the animal I received. You don't necessarily have to tell the person about the animal they remind you of. It is just a way to find out attributes they may have.

You can use any category. For instance, fruits and vegetables, types of automobiles, etc. The categories are endless. These are just fun ways to get the prophetic flowing. You could start with this phrase, "You remind me of the kind of person that would..." and then just keep saying whatever you get. These simple activations are not only fun, they are also really great to get the prophetic currents flowing. You can even do prophetic games with your friends and family by writing categories on little strips of paper and then partnering up and prophesying over each other using a certain category. So be creative and get your prophetic muscles pumping.

Let's see how this would look in action. Suppose I am walking around Wal-Mart and I notice a lady that looks discouraged. I want to bring her some kingdom encouragement, so I ask the Holy Spirit if there is anything He has for her. If I don't sense any revelation coming, I ask internally, "Holy Spirit, what kind of animal is she like?" Let's say I see a mental image of a big black momma bear. I will start thinking about what attributes a mother bear has, especially allowing the Holy Spirit to help me with this. I think of how protective a momma bear is, and how she would risk her life for her children.

I feel like I am to share with this lady what I have so far. I approach her and say something like, "Excuse me, but I wanted to say that I really feel like you are a great mom. I feel like you are super protective like a momma bear and that God really loves you." As I share that, I see a number three in my mind and I feel it has to do with the number of children she has. I say, "I saw the number three. Do you have three children?" She says, "Yes, I do. You are freaking me out. Who are you?" Then another prophetic tissue pops up. I feel a pain in my lower back and ask her if she has lower back pain.

As I say that, I have a mental vision of her left leg growing out.

"She says, "Yes, I do have lower back pain." I look over and see a bench and I tell her, "The reason your lower back hurts is because I believe your left leg is shorter than your right one." She sits down and I test out the length of her legs. Sure enough, her left leg is shorter. We pray and Jesus grows it out. This is a make-believe situation, but this is really how the supernatural and prophetic flow together.

YOU REMIND ME OF SOMEONE

A common way God speaks prophetically is when someone reminds you of someone else that you know. If I see a random person, and I have a thought that they remind me of my friend John, I would think to myself, "What is it about John that I am thinking about right now?" My thoughts are, "John is really funny and a great team player."

Many times God is communicating that this random person you do not know probably has similar gifts, personality or strengths of the person you thought of. The next time this happens to you, try this: Go up to person you see and ask them, "Hello, I just had to say, you really remind me of my friend 'so and so.' This is what is amazing about my friend." Then describe the great attributes of your friend. Let the person know that you believe they may have those same strengths too. That is why God pointed them out to you. You can ask them if that makes sense to them.

You might be wondering, "But what if I get it wrong?"

I'm so glad you asked this important question. The bottom line is this. If we swing and miss, but we are motivated by love we are not wrong. The details may be incorrect but we are right that we took a chance to step out to love someone. Love never fails.

TWO WRONGS MAKE A RIGHT

Here is a fun testimony of when I missed the prophetic target and God showed up any way. We were on a ministry trip in Southern California, having lunch in a nearby Mexican restaurant. The group was our ministry team and some people from the church where we were ministering. I felt a pain in my right shoulder, so I asked everyone at our table if anyone there had a right shoulder problem. No one responded. Then the assistant pastor's wife said that her left shoulder--not her right one--had been bothering her for years. She said the pain level was around an eight out of ten, ten being the worst. She also could not raise her elbow above her head. We prayed and she received fifty per cent improvement. We prayed again and Jesus healed her shoulder one hundred per cent. Come on!

Then my right hip had a sharp pain. I asked, "Who has right hip pain?" Another lady from their church said, "My left hip--not my right one--is in constant pain." My friend Ben checked her legs out in a chair and her left leg was three-fourths of an inch shorter than her right leg. They prayed as the owner of the restaurant looked on. Jesus grew her leg out for everyone to see and all the pain left her hip. She tested it out by doing awkward looking contortions, and she declared, "There is no more pain!"

The restaurant owner said to Ben, "Can you do anything about this?" She showed Ben her crippled hand. She said that it was crippling arthritis, and she couldn't open and close her hand. Her hand was mostly stuck in a semi-closed position. She said, "I cannot use this hand for anything anymore." Ben said, "Yes, Jesus can heal that!" He then commanded her hand to work in Jesus' name. She slowly started to open and close her hand. She said she was feeling heat in it. She started getting really excited as the mobility in her hand increased.

Within a few moments, her once crippled, locked up hand had complete mobility and was pain free. She picked up some pans showing everyone how Jesus had healed her. This restaurant owner has since sent many people to the church where we were ministering. Any time she overhears her customers complaining of sickness, she sends them down the street to the church to be healed. All this started with two of my swings that missed their mark. But the Holy Spirit didn't miss; He hit a home run!

WORD OF KNOWLEDGE

"Now to each one the manifestation of the Spirit is given for the common good. To one there is given through the Spirit a message of wisdom, to another a word of knowledge by means of the same Spirit, to another faith by the same Spirit, to another gifts of healing by that one Spirit, to another miraculous powers, to another prophecy, to another distinguishing between spirits, to another speaking in different kinds of tongues, and to still another the interpretation of tongues. All these are the work of one and the same Spirit, and he distributes them to each one, just

as he determines" (1 Corinthians 12:7-11 NIV).

A word of knowledge (w.o.k.) is a supernatural detail or insight about a person's life, an event, or circumstance, either present or past tense. It can be insight into a problem to find a solution, like a formula for an invention. Prophecy can be futuristic, but words of knowledge are not. They are current or past tense facts. You can answer a w.o.k. question with a yes or no. If I asked if your name was John, the answer is either yes or no. If I asked if you were born in July or if you had two sisters, the answer would be yes or no. If I see a Mexican flag over you, and you are from Mexico, that would be a w.o.k. If I see a Mexican flag over you, and you aren't from Mexico, it could have a prophetic futuristic meaning. You may develop a heart for Mexico someday, although you are unaware of that now.

Prophecy can sometimes be subjective in nature since it can be for future events, but words of knowledge are objective facts. That is one reason words of knowledge are so powerful in ministry. When God gives you supernatural insight into people's current life situations, it really impacts them. It can unlock the hardest and coldest heart when you get a specific detail about their life.

BRITTANY AT BURGER KING

One day I was going through a Burger King drive-through. As I was pulling up to order, I heard the name "Brittany" in my heart. As I was paying for my food I asked if anyone named Brittany was there. The young lady said, "Yes, there is. I'll go get her." She brought Brittany to the drive through window. When she looked at me she told the drive-through girl that it must be

---

another Brittany because she didn't know me. I got Brittany's attention and she came up to the window. I said, "I know you don't know me, but as I was pulling in, I heard the name Brittany in my heart. I felt I was supposed to talk to you." She gave me a really shocked and confused look as the Lord started showing me other things in her heart.

I said, "I feel you are wanting to go back to college, but you kind of feel stuck. God is going to help you with that." The other girl asked if I had anything from God for her. God gave me some details into her life too. As I grabbed my food, Brittany asked if I could pull up front because she wanted to take her break and talk to me more. I pulled around front and Brittany and three other girls came out to meet me. They all asked if I could pray for them. I prophesied over them all. Then we joined hands and all four girls gave their lives back to Jesus. Brittany told me that her friends had recently been talking to her about becoming New Age. She had told Jesus last night that she wasn't sure if she believed in Him anymore. The night before she had prayed, "God, if Jesus is God, could you please show me." She told me through a huge grin, "Now I know for sure that Jesus is God!"

REVISIT CHAPTER 5

You may want to revisit Chapter 5 on revelation before we move on. It may help to review the ways that revelation comes, because words of knowledge come through the same ways we discussed in Chapter 5. The more common ways words of knowledge come for physical healing are feeling impressions on your body, seeing a mental picture of a body part or having an internal knowing of an injury. Having a random memory flashback of a certain disease or a past specific miracle is usually God communicating to you that there is someone around you now that needs that same healing. The best way to grow in getting accurate words of knowledge is just to practice. Try to get a word of knowledge for someone and then ask him or her if you are right. You will never know if you are right until you actually ask. I will talk about keys to courage later on in this book to help you with stepping out in more boldness. I guarantee that if you practice getting words of knowledge, you will get them. The Holy Spirit desires to give you words of knowledge more than you want to get them.

There is an increased measure of faith for healing that is released in a word of knowledge. When a word of knowledge is released, there is a grace and an anointing to empower it. It is similar to the prophetic when the blue God words join our red words. Words of knowledge that hit the mark are purple. Many times when you get a word of knowledge that hits the mark, you do not even need to pray. If I asked someone "Do you have a problem in your left knee?" If they say yes, I might declare, "Test it out right now. Move it around. God is already healing it." Many times the power for the healing accompanies the specific word of knowledge.

 **ACTION STEP**

- Watch Video #8A - Basic Prophecy

Physical Healing

"Live in such a way that unless God shows up, what you're attempting to do is bound to fail. This is the nature of the Gospel." – Bill Johnson

Joaquin Evans, who helped pioneer the Bethel healing rooms, shared a truth during a healing school that changed the way I view healing. He said, "God is not just the healer, but He is healing." God Himself is healing. Joaquin shared that when the Lord showed him this, he had the epiphany that his job was not to try to get people healed, but to cultivate and host God's presence. As God's presence is cultivated and welcomed, people will be healed in God's manifest presence, because God is healing. This is awesome! It points back to keeping the main thing the main thing. Draw close to God and learn to cultivate His presence around your life. This thing is so simple!

Miracles are God's Love Language

I have yet to see someone healed that didn't feel God's love directed toward them afterward. I have witnessed dogmatic atheists come to Jesus after they were healed. He is irresistibly good. Healing is God's love being poured out into the world. It demonstrates His love and goodness. Our job is to fully preach the gospel. People are free to choose what they do with it. Jesus died so that everyone could be saved. It is a free gift to all. Healing is also a free gift to the world.

People ask me often, "Jason, when you minister healing to the sick do you pray from authority or are you being led by the Holy Spirit?"

Some believe that we pray only from authority from the Word of God. Others will not pray for the sick unless they feel a supernatural impression from the Holy Spirit. I believe we should experience both. Jesus gave us all power and authority to heal every sickness and disease (Luke 10:19). When I pray for the sick, my foundation in healing is always rooted in the place of authority in His Word. If the Holy Spirit gives me a specific insight, I will follow His lead. If I do not get a specific leading I stand in the authority of the written Word. I view it like being married and having a marriage contract. The contract is the authority of that marriage. It is the legally binding document.

We have a legally binding contract to heal the sick. That is the authority that I stand on. But a marriage is much more than a legal contract. It is a living relationship with a real person. When my best friend, Holy Spirit, gives me some prophetic insight, I choose to go with it because of my relationship with Him. He is God and knows how to heal better than I do. If I do not get any specific insight, I will command the sickness to go as a normal prayer model. If the Holy Spirit shows me something specific I take note of that, switch gears with Him and do as He leads me.

Now let's cover some basic prayer models. These are tools to help get you started in your supernatural journey. Please do not get stuck in a certain method or formula. Jesus did not use cookie cutter healing prayer models. As you read the Bible, it is apparent that He rarely healed the same way twice. Stay close to the Holy Spirit's leading and His presence. Pray from your authority in Christ founded on the Word of God. Before we cover some basic healing prayer models I want to share this fun testimony from Mexico.

BROCCOLI AND CHEESE MIRACLES

On a mission trip to Mexico some BSSM students ran low on translators. During the healing time, the students that didn't have translators just sat as spectators on the stage. There was a massive amount of people in the crowd waiting for prayer, but there were only a handful of translators. One third year BSSM leader saw that much of his ministry team was not praying for the sick. He called the whole ministry team to a quick team huddle and told them, "It doesn't matter whether or not you can speak or understand Spanish. The Holy Spirit knows what He is doing and He will flow through you even if you have no idea what the people's prayer needs are."

This leader had some people from the crowd that needed healing to come onto the stage. The leader said, "To prove to you that it makes no difference what words you use to heal the sick, I will have you say 'broccoli and cheese' over this man's bad back." So that is all they prayed, "Broccoli and cheese," and the man's back was instantly healed. They moved to another lady with a deaf ear and the leader had them pray, "Mashed potatoes and gravy," and the lady's deaf ear opened! The team was released to pray through the masses of people having no translators. Just like the third year leader said, words and understanding were not important. What was important was that the Holy Spirit was with them and He performed incredible miracles through them. Blind eyes opened and the deaf heard as they just walked through the crowds and touched people saying, "Broccoli and cheese" and "mashed potatoes and gravy."

Randy Clark was asked, "When did you see the greatest break-through in healing?" He replied, "When I finally realized that I have nothing to do with it."

Ministering Healing

Initial Interview

It is a good idea to do an initial interview before you pray. Medical doctors do this too. Ask the person what their pain level is on a scale from zero to ten, with ten being excruciating pain and zero being none. Also, ask them if they have any limited mobility, and see what the range of motion is before you pray. Now you have a good starting reference point to measure what happens through the healing.

A Basic Prayer Model

Always ask permission before you lay hands on people. You can pray without touching them too.

Guys should only touch a lady on their shoulders or have them put their hand on the pain and then put your hand over theirs. It is better to have ladies lay hands on ladies and guys on guys for obvious reasons. Be gender appropriate.

Release the Holy Spirit's presence on them and use short command prayers. This is not time to talk to God about their sickness. It is time to talk to the sickness about God. Speak directly to the sickness and pain as if it were a person and command it to go! Use short commands like, "Holy Spirit, come," "Left knee be healed in Jesus' name," "I command you, pain, to come out!"

DECLARATION PRAYER

This type of prayer is very effective. It is declaring what God is already doing. It sounds like this: "The power of God is healing your left knee right now, so move it around. What's happening?"

PROPHETIC ACTS

This is having the person act out something that the Holy Spirit is showing you. My friend, Taylor, was praying for a man that was missing a thumb bone. He prayed several times and nothing happened. Then he thought of the story of Moses in Exodus 4:

> "Then the Lord said, 'Put your hand inside your cloak.' So Moses put his hand into his cloak, and when he took it out, it was leprous, like snow. 'Now put it back into your cloak,' he said. So Moses put his hand back into his cloak, and when he took it out, it was restored, like the rest of his flesh." (Exodus 4:6-7)

So Taylor asked this man missing the thumb bone to put his hand in his jacket pocket and then pull it out. When he pulled it out the first time, he felt a small lump that had grown. My friend then told him, "That's a new bone. Put your hand back in your pocket." He put his hand in his pocket and then took it out again. The hard lump had grown bigger. On the third time, the man had a brand new thumb bone.

SHADOW HEALING

> "As a result, people brought the sick into the streets and laid them on beds and mats so that at least Peter's

shadow might fall on some of them as he passed by"
(Acts 5:15 NIV).

These people were healed as Peter's shadow touched them. There is no inherent power in a shadow. It was the overshadowing of the Holy Spirit that healed these people.

> *"The Holy Spirit will come upon you, and the power of the Most High will overshadow you"* (Luke 1:35 NIV).

I have seen many people healed by our shadow, overshadowed by the Holy Spirit. We will move our shadow over the area in their bodies that needs healing and then have them test it out.

LONG DISTANCE MIRACLES

God can heal from any distance. There is no time and space in the spirit realm. Miracles can happen just as easily over the phone, the Internet or by praying from a far away distance. *"He sent forth his word and healed them..."* (Psalm 107:20). We celebrated a lady's crooked leg being lengthened and healed over Skype last year, and she was in Pakistan. She walked around without her cane, no longer limping because Jesus Christ had healed her!

SUSIE'S MOM - LONG DISTANCE CANCER HEALING

My friend Alexander was on a Treasure Hunt with a BSSM first year student. They went to the mall and found one of my friends named Susie. She was wearing a red shirt and they had red shirt as a clue on their treasure map. Alexander had never

---

met Susie before and didn't know she was a friend of mine. Alexander and the girl introduced themselves, then somewhere in the conversation, Alexander mentioned that he was my housemate. They asked Susie if she had any prayer needs. Susie told them that her mom who was named Mercedes needed prayer. Alexander remembered having a random clue of a car's name on his map. Alexander looked at his map and showed Susie that clue and explained that her mom's name Mercedes is a car's name.

They asked Susie if her mom needed prayer for anything. Susie told them, "My mother is in real bad shape. She has stage-four cancer throughout her entire body and has been sent home to die. The doctors have tried their best, but there is nothing left they can do for her. They have sent Mercedes home to die." Susie said that her mom had been bedridden for a while and lately her mom did not even have enough strength to talk to anyone on the phone. The doctors had asked the family to say their last goodbyes to Mercedes. Susie had just returned from saying goodbye to her mom who lived eight hours away. In the middle of the mall, they prayed with Susie for her mom that Jesus would destroy that cancer in her body.

"For this purpose the Son of God was manifested, that he might destroy the works of the devil" (1 John 3:8).

A few months later I saw Susie at the mall. I walked up to her and she shared this story with me: "A while back, your friend Alexander and a girl prayed for my mom. She was on her death-bed and in the final throes of it. I have to tell you what Jesus did. It is absolutely incredible! Shortly after we prayed in the mall, my mom called me. She hadn't had the strength to talk on the phone before, but she called me and said, "Susie, I don't know how to explain this, but I woke up this morning with so much strength and energy in my body. I couldn't stay in that bed any longer, so I got up and started cleaning my house. Susie, I do not know where this energy is coming from." Susie told Mercedes about how they had prayed for her from the mall. Susie said, "Mom, you have to go back to the doctor and have them check you out."

Susie told me that her mother went back to the doctor. He ran multiple tests on Mercedes just because he couldn't believe the results they were getting. Those reports kept saying there was not one single strand of cancer in her body. They could not find any cancer! She was healed by the great power of the Holy Spirit! The doctor told the family, "In over twenty years of practicing medicine, I has never seen anything like this. This is truly a miracle!"

I had Alexander review this testimony for my book to make sure that I had all the details accurate. He told me, "Jason, what is funny about this testimony is I still remember that day so clearly. I remember how much I didn't want to Treasure Hunt that day. The only reason I went was because I was in charge of leading Treasure Hunts that week. I only went because there was this first year BSSM student that needed someone to go with her. Driving home, I was thinking that today was probably the worst Treasure Hunt I had ever been on. We hadn't seen one single person get healed." Alexander didn't hear about Mercedes radical healing of cancer until months later when I bumped into Susie and came home and told him. We don't always get to see the impact of our love in action.

PRAYER CLOTHS

"So that even handkerchiefs and aprons that had touched him were taken to the sick, and their illnesses were cured and the evil spirits left them" (Acts19:12 NIV).

Sometimes we will pray over prayer cloths and family members will take the these anointed clothes home to a sick relative. People will be miraculously healed as these prayer cloths touch them. I personally have been involved with a young man that had one hundred per cent blindness and was healed as a prayer cloth was put on his eyes. This happened at UC Davis hospital.

THE POWER OF JOY

I have seen some of the most dramatic miracles as joy was released through laughter. *"In Your presence is fullness of joy..."* (Psalm 16:11). When God's presence shows up, joy happens. Joy is also a conduit of the kingdom. Miracles happen easily in His joy. Laughter releases joy.

"The kingdom of God is...righteousness, peace and joy in the Holy Spirit" (Romans 14:17).

One third of the kingdom is joy. Joy is a huge portion of our Christian life. Jesus was the happiest miracle worker around.

*"Therefore God, your God, has anointed you (Jesus)
with the oil of gladness more than your companions"*
(Psalm 45:7).

Psalm 2:4 says, *"The One enthroned in heaven laughs; the Lord
scoffs at them."* The context is the Lord scoffing at the plans of the
enemy. I believe God is sitting in heaven and laughing at the enemy's
plans to kill, steal and destroy. Jesus said, *"I tell you the truth, the
Son...does only what he sees the Father doing. Whatever the Father
does, the Son also does."* (John 5:19). I'm sure Jesus saw His Father
sitting on the throne laughing at the plans of the enemy. Sickness
and disease are part of the enemy's plan, so it is okay to laugh and
scoff at them. Ha ha ha!

Kenneth E. Hagin, known as a father of the faith movement,
shares a personal testimony of resisting the devil through joy.

I was holding a meeting for a friend of mine a
number of years ago when I was awakened at 1:30 in
the morning by alarming symptoms in my body. (I
knew something about them because I'd been born
with a deformed heart and became bedfast from it.
Doctors had said I could die at any minute, but I was
healed by the power of God when I was 17.) These
severe symptoms were in the region of my heart and
chest. The devil said to my mind, "Uh-huh, you're
going to die. That's exactly what's going to happen
to you. You're lucky you've gotten this far. Remember what the doctors said?" (That sounds like him,
doesn't it?) "This is one time you're not going to get
your healing," he kept repeating like a voice speak-

ing to my mind. "Now it's all come back, and you're going to die. In fact, you're dying now. Somebody asked me, "What did you do?"

Well, it was in the wintertime, so I pulled the covers up over my head and started laughing. Now, I didn't feel like laughing. There is such a thing as laughter inspired by the Spirit of God where you just can't help it, but I put this one on. I made myself do it. I covered my head (because I didn't want to wake up the rest of the folks in the house) and laughed out loud. It seems to me I must have laughed about 10 minutes. Finally the devil said, "What are you laughing about?" I said, "I'm laughing at you, because you said I'm not going to get healed." "That's right," he said, "This is one time you're not going to healed." I said, "Ha, ha, ha, ha, ha, ha, ha, ha, ha, ha, ha, ha, ha." (I just made myself do it.) I went on and on and on. Finally the devil said for the third time, "What are you laughing about?" I said, "I've already told you. I'll tell you again: I'm laughing at you." "What are you laughing at me about?" "You said I'm not going to get healed." "That's right. This is one time you're not going to get your *healing.*"

I said, "Ha, ha, Mr. Devil. Sure, I'm not going to get it. What do I need to get it for? Jesus already got it for me! I don't need to get it. All I have to do is accept it. Now, in case you can't read," I said, "I'll just quote 1 Peter 2:24 to you. It says, 'Who his own self bore our sins in his own body on the tree, that we, being dead to sins, should live onto righteousness: by whose stripes ye WERE healed.' "If we were, I was. So I don't have to get it; Jesus already got it for me, and because He got it for me, I accept it, claim it, and have it. Now you just gather up your little symptoms and get out of here." You never saw anybody scurry about, gather up their belongings, and take off as fast in your life.[1]

Kenneth Hagin says when he learned about divine healing, he personally was never sick in over 60 years.

Kevin Dedmon, a pastor at Bethel Church, had someone's thumb that was cut off grow back in his hand. The entire thumb had been cut off with just a little nub left. Jesus grew a brand new thumb out as Kevin released God's good mood over it though laughter. All he did was laugh as he held on to this nub. Kevin says he was laughing at thinking how impossible it is to grow a new thumb. After a few minutes, God had grown a new thumb! God asks us to do the impossible. This testimony of God's goodness makes me happy.

As you can see, there are so many ways to release healing and these are just a few. At a conference Pete Cabrera, Jr. and I were discussing several ways that the Bible records how people were healed. There is the prayer of faith, the anointing, the healing atmosphere, our authority, gifts of healing, prophetic acts, God's name, angels, and the list keeps going on. It is as if God is saying to us, "I will give you so many avenues to heal the sick that you will realize every believer can do this. No one is excluded from healing the sick and you can't mess it up."

TEST OUT WHAT IS HAPPENING

After you release healing make sure to have them test it out. Have them tell you what the pain level and mobility are now. Compare that with the original number and mobility they gave you during the initial interview. Focus on any improvement that you see. If the pain was at a nine and now it is an eight, something is happening! Let them know God is doing something even if the pain went down ten per cent. Give thanks for any improvement. Whatever we give thanks for will multiply. Focus on what God is doing, not on what hasn't happened yet. Jesus didn't have enough fish to feed the five thousand, but He gave thanks anyway. When Jesus did this, it released the principle of thanksgiving, which is multiplication, and God brought the increase. So give thanks and pray again. You will see the most amazing results as you do this.

HOW MANY TIMES SHOULD I PRAY?

Pray as many times as needed until they are healed, or until they need to go. I ask the Holy Spirit for insight while praying. I pray until I feel the grace lift, then I will usually ask to pray one more time. I have seen radical miracles after the eighth time praying and others after the first time. The main focus is on helping people get better, so if they have time, so do I. I know God's will is to heal them, so I will take as much time as they allow me to. Jesus prayed more than once for a blind man to receive his sight.

> *"Then He came to Bethsaida; and they brought a blind man to Him, and begged Him to touch him. So He took the blind man by the hand and led him out of the town. And when He had spit on his eyes*

and put His hands on him, He asked him if he saw anything. And he looked up and said, 'I see men like trees, walking.' Then He put His hands on his eyes again and made him look up. And he was restored and saw everyone clearly" (Mark 8:22-25).

Partner with what God is doing by asking them questions like, "What is happening with you? What are you experiencing right now?" Sometimes the Holy Spirit is doing something completely different than what we are focusing on in the moment. Say you are praying for a man's shoulder. When you ask him what he is feeling, he says, "My stomach is on fire!" You find out that he had a stomach hernia that you didn't know about. When you ask him to check out the hernia, he says that the lump is gone.

Say you are praying for a lady with arthritic pain and you ask her what is happening and she says, "Nothing really, I just started thinking about my ex-husband that cheated on me fifteen years ago." Pay attention to those things. The Holy Spirit is most likely moving on her heart to forgive her ex-husband. Once she forgives him, the pain will probably leave immediately. That arthritic infirmity is in all likelihood lodged in her pain and unforgiveness. The body, soul and spirit in a human are very interconnected. Physical healing can bring emotional healing. Spiritual deliverance can bring a physical healing. Emotional pain can bring physical pain. So emotional freedom can affect freedom for their body too.

In Illinois, a young lady with eyeglasses stood before us for healing. She had a long list of healing needs. She said "I have multiple sclerosis, lupus, a broken tail bone, trouble sleeping and..." She mentioned several other physical ailments that I do not recall. As she was telling us her list of needs, I heard the Holy Spirit say, "She is very hard and critical on herself. She needs to forgive herself." I asked her if what I heard from the Holy Spirit was true. She said, "Yes," and immediately started to tremble and sob. We led her in a forgiveness prayer. "I choose to forgive myself for anything that I have done intentionally or unintentionally in my life. I forgive myself for things that I failed to do and I release myself from any punishment now in Jesus' name!" When she did this all of her physical symptoms left. The pain in her tailbone disappeared, and she said that she felt a lightness inside. She took off her glasses, saying "I can't see through these now." God was healing her eye sight, too. A few weeks later we got the good news back. She had gone to the doctor. The test results said she no longer had multiple sclerosis, lupus or any of the other diseases. She had received her freedom in Jesus' name!

Partner with the Holy Spirit, because He knows what He is doing. He is the best ministry partner. He was alongside Jesus performing every single miracle of the Bible. He is here with us. Spend time getting to know Him and setting people free.

What If They Only Get Partially Healed?

What if the person you are praying for has to leave and they are not one hundred percent healed in that moment? First, let me explain the difference between miracles and healing. Miracles are one hundred percent instant. Healing is progressive. If I do not see an instant miracle, then I tell the person the difference between an instant miracle and a progressive healing. I encourage them to pay attention and give thanks for any improvement that they see in the next day or two. I will usually share a quick testimony of someone that was healed progressively over a couple of days. There is power in sharing a previous testimony of someone getting healed. We will cover this amazing principle later on in the chapter. I leave them with a prophetic word of encouragement saying how much Jesus loves them. I want them to feel loved by God and me. We can minister without love, but every time we love someone is ministered to.

HOKEY POKEY HEALING

My friends Kristina, Alexander, Paul and I went to the Sundial Bridge to release revival through the Hokey Pokey. We felt the Holy Spirit say to go to the Sundial Bridge, and He would heal people using the Hokey Pokey. We also felt like a right elbow would be healed and someone that worked at a car lot or car dealership would have a radical love encounter. The first person we saw on the bridge was a fifty year-old security guard. We did the Hokey Pokey with him and his right knee was healed around fifty percent. Smiling, he thanked us and said, "It has been years since I had done the Hokey Pokey."

Halfway down the bridge, a couple approached us. We asked them if they would like to do the Hokey Pokey with us. The young man said to his pregnant girlfriend, "I think we should." We all got in a circle and did the Hokey Pokey. "You put your left arm in…You put your left arm out…you put your left arm in and you shake it all about…" We got so happy from God's presence while doing the Hokey Pokey that the young man asked, "Are you guys on crack or something?" We said, "No, we're on something much better!"

Then we asked them if they had any problems with their physical bodies and if so to test it out and to see if they were healed. The girl bent completely backwards saying, "My back is better. I couldn't do that before!" The young man started moving his right elbow up and down saying, "This is crazy, my elbow always pops and hurts. It isn't popping right now, and it doesn't hurt anymore! This is so weird." We explained how Jesus had told us He wanted to heal people tonight at the Sundial Bridge and He wanted to use the Hokey Pokey.

We then started sharing some prophetic words that we were getting for them. We said to the young man, "We see you working on cars and you are really good at it." Shocked, he looked down at his clothes and said, "I work at a car dealership as a mechanic! How do you know that? I'm not even in my uniform." We shared that God had showed us his occupation, so that he could know that God sees him and loves him very much. We got to pray and release God's presence and love over the couple, and also prayed destiny over the unborn baby. They hugged us and said, "We really needed this tonight. You have no idea!" They said they had both asked Jesus in their lives before, and we encouraged them to keep going to Jesus.

A couple of months later, my friend Naomi and I were giving new socks away to the poor and praying for people. On that day, we saw Jesus heal a man that was about seventy percent blind. He was so happy that he could now read his Bible. Come on, Jesus! As we were giving away these socks, Naomi shared this with me, "Jason, today at work my co-worker heard that I was going out today to give away socks and pray for people. My co-worker asked me if I was part of the group that does the Hokey Pokey on the Sundial Bridge. Naomi told him no, but that her friends were the ones who had done that.

Naomi's co-worker said, "My friend and his girlfriend were at the Sundial Bridge one night and a group of people asked him if they wanted to do the Hokey Pokey with them. They decided to, and my friend said that his right elbow was completely healed that night. He told me that he didn't really believe it was healed at the time, and he was waiting for the popping and the pain to come back every day since then. That was months ago and it never did come back. My friend was a high school football star, and he has been telling everyone for weeks how God had healed his right elbow doing the Hokey Pokey on the Sundial Bridge. He has been telling all his friends and family of this God miracle!"

THE POWER OF THE TESTIMONY

"For the testimony of Jesus is the spirit of prophecy" (Revelation 19:10).

Bill Johnson has unveiled, stewarded and propelled an amazing supernatural principle called the power of the testimony. He gets this revelation from Revelation 19:10 *"For the testimony of Jesus is the spirit of prophecy."* He uncovers that the primitive root for the Hebrew word testimony used here means "to duplicate or to repeat." It literally means, "to do it again." Remember that prophecy has the creative power to change a current event immediately into something it wasn't before the prophetic word was spoken. When we speak a testimony of what Jesus has done in the past, there is actually power released in the spirit saying, "Do it again". There is an anointing released into the atmosphere to duplicate or repeat in that moment the same testimony Jesus did.

Bill shares an incredible chain of events of several children being healed of clubbed feet just through the power of the testimony. It started with a young boy named Chris who was healed of severe clubbed feet while at Bethel Church. He ran for the very first time after he was healed in the prayer line. Later, Bill was teaching about the power of the testimony, and shared the story of the little boy Chris that was healed of clubbed feet. A mother that had a two year-old daughter with clubbed feet in the nursery listened to the testimony of Chris being healed and the principle of the power of the testimony, meaning that God wants to "do it again." She said in her heart, "I'll take that for my daughter." After the service was over, she went to the nursery and her daughter's clubbed feet were already straightened out perfectly. No one had prayed for her daughter. It had happened through the power of the testimony being released when the girl's mother said, "I will take that for my daughter."

When Bill was in North Carolina, he shared this teaching about the power of the testimony and a lady was watching over live-streaming from Brazil. Her daughter was around ten years old and had severely deformed crooked feet. She was a beautiful young girl, but everyone would stare at her deformed feet. She was very humiliated and insecure because of the deformity. When the mother heard the testimony of Chris, the healing of two-year-old girl, and the principle about the power of the testimony, she called for her daughter to come to her. She told her daughter to take off her shoes. As the daughter walked towards the mother, her feet straightened perfectly right before her eyes.

I have friends that travel the world doing miracle services. The main way they break open the atmosphere for miracles is to share lots of past miracle testimonies. These testimonies of Jesus prophesy to the atmosphere, "Do it again!" Miracles sometimes happen as the testimony is released without any form of prayer at all. They will share a story of a lady's deaf ear that was healed in Israel. Then someone in that audience will jump up and say, "My deaf ear just popped open!" Jesus is amazing!

"THIS ISN'T GOING TO WORK!"

I was in Chicago training at a School of the Supernatural. We taught for about an hour, and then went to the streets to show God in action. Our group of about ten arrived at one of the roughest parts of town. Outside McDonald's in the street, a fight was about to break out. I could hardly believe what was transpiring before us. There was a group of guys on each side of the street yelling and threatening each other. A gal was actually initiating one group and calling out threats to another man that was the leader of the other group. The gal seemed to be the most upset. There were about six to eight people in each group. I was sure it was about to escalate into physical violence.

I asked God, "What should we do?" Instantly I heard two polar opposite voices in my head. One said, "Jump right in the middle of this because the Gospel has to be proven!" The other voice said, "You have people with you that you are responsible for...Don't do anything!" The tension inside of me escalated, as did the hostility in the street. In that moment I looked to my team and said, "I am going in. You stay here if you like." Two gals followed me. One gal named Nancy had seemed really timid and quiet during the training, so I was surprised that she followed me. Along with her, Donna, a very strong outgoing type, came too.

We walked up to the hostile group and I shouted, "Jesus is here! He has healed several people today and He is here now to do the same. Does anybody here have pain in their back and need prayer?" A confused look came across the bunch and two girls on the sidewalk responded saying they both had pain in their backs. In that moment, the ringleader gal walked away and the angry group dissipated. I thought to myself, "Wow, this really works!"

The girls that needed prayer said their pain level was around a seven out of ten. I asked the two girls with me to pray for them, but Nancy shook her head and said, "No, you pray for her!" I smiled back at Nancy and said, "You got this. Just keep the prayer short." With a look on her face that said, "I can't believe you're making me do this!" she closed her eyes and started praying silently. After about ten seconds, I interrupted their prayers and said, "Check out your backs, move them around. What's happening?" Both gals with the back pain said in unison, "There's no pain! My back doesn't hurt at all." The look on Nancy's face was priceless. It was a roller coaster of facial expressions I would interpret as saying, "I think they are lying...Did I really just heal somebody?...Wow! This is amazing!...No, it can't be this easy... They definitely are faking it!" I wish I had my video camera to catch all the thoughts and emotions that were so apparently running through Nancy's brain.

On the way back to church, I eagerly asked Nancy, "So what was happening when you were praying for the ladies' backs?" Her answer pleasantly and completely surprised me. She said, "I wasn't praying, but I was saying to myself, 'This isn't going to work...This isn't going to work...What am I doing?...This isn't going to work!'"

How could this be possible? Who had the faith to be healed in that situation? The gals on the street receiving prayer didn't have any faith. The only faith Nancy had was strong negative faith and professed doubt. So how in the world could God move in a situation like that where there is no faith for healing?

I'll tell you who had enough faith in that moment: God. God has great faith in His love for people. He has an Almighty trump card in His hand called LOVE. The Bible says *"And now these three remain: faith, hope and love. But the greatest of these is love"* (1 Corinthians 13:13).

I would be foolish to say that faith plays no part in healing, but I also know I would be foolish to ignore the fact that my Father has a trump card called LOVE. His love can always take up the gap in my lack of faith or anyone else's. We all grow in measures of our faith, but remember love never fails. Trust that God's love for people is greater than any faith or doubt that you may have as you step out to love others. Put your faith in His love.

ENDNOTES

1.   Source: *How to Keep Your Healing* by Kenneth E. Hagin
       Excerpt permission granted by Faith Library Publications.

 ## ACTION STEPS

- Watch Video #8B - Healing the Sick

Chapter 9

Keys to Courage

"What are you saving yourself for? In your lifetime, you can either leave a big mark in the earth or you can go out with a whimper. The choice is yours...Son, what are you going to do?" –Joyce Berry, my mom

I am convinced that most believers have an inner desire to reach out to love people around them. If Jesus lives in our hearts, and God is love, then it is the most natural response to want to help others. It is fear and intimidation that tries to keep us from loving others. The devil doesn't mind it so much when we stay in our bedrooms locked away praying for revival. But what the enemy will try to stop you through intimidation is sharing your faith in public. We pray for revival and for a great move of God. That is a powerful and necessary part of revival, but only part. Intercessory prayer MUST be accompanied with action, miracles and deliverance in the marketplace. The gospel must be preached and demonstrated in power for the kingdom of God to be established.

It's interesting to me what Jesus said after the seventy-two returned from doing His work in the marketplace: Healing the sick and casting out demons. Jesus said, *"I saw Satan fall like lightning from heaven"* (Luke 10:18). Satan did not fall from heaven during the rallied prayer meeting. He fell as he was being dethroned from individual people's lives through physical healing and spiritual deliverance. Satan is dethroned when God's kingdom invades real people's situations all around us. That is why one of the enemy's greatest ploys is to keep us inside our homes to pray at a distance for others.

I will not lie. It can feel scary to approach others with the Gospel of Jesus for many reasons. That is why everyone does not do it. But God has called us to be giant killers! In this chapter I will share some keys that helped me step past fear into courage. Bill Johnson says, "Without fear there would be no courage." Kris Vallotton says, "It is the dogs of doom that stand at your doorway of destiny." When you feel fear that means the doorway to your supernatural destiny is somewhere close by.

Much of the favor and breakthrough on my life has been in learning how to live a consistent and persistent lifestyle of reaching out to love others in public. I have learned about resistance and momentum while growing in the miraculous. When beginning your supernatural journey, it is like trying to get a railway locomotive rolling. It takes more energy and output to get it rolling from a complete standstill. Once it starts moving, it takes less effort and power to increase momentum. It is the same in the supernatural. It takes more courage to take that first step to reach out to others, but once you are moving, even if barely rolling forward, it gets easier with each step. Once this train is moving full speed ahead, it is hard to stop. Likewise, we do not want to start this lifestyle and stop. We are in this for life! It is not a one-time a year outreach event we are called to. It is a lifelong lifestyle of reaching out to love others with Jesus. Our life is meant to be the outreach. The keys in this chapter are to help you get the train rolling from a standstill and then to keep the momentum going and growing.

Encouragement

I have found that encouragement is one of the major sources of fuel that keeps us going. There is a story of encouragement that I really like. Judges 20:21 states that in one day, 22,000 Israelite men were cut down with the sword in battle. It was a devastating loss. Talk about a bad day! I'm sure great discouragement and fear entered the hearts of the Israelite camp. I can only imagine how these men felt like giving up and giving in, but in verse 22 it says,

> *"But the people, the men of Israel, took courage (taking heart again) and again formed the battle line in the same place where they had formed it on the first day"* (Judges 20:22).

They took up their battle positions as on the first day. They set up their line of attack as they did before their great defeat. This is HUGE! They basically said, "We are going to believe and have courage as we did before our great defeat yesterday. We are going to do this again!" They positioned their hearts once again to believe God to do great exploits through them. I believe they reminded each other of past testimonies of God's power and victory and how He would do it again. They encouraged themselves, and it was that courage that enabled them to position themselves for God's victory. The Bible records that the Israelites went out in battle as on the first day and they annihilated the army that was before them and had a tremendous victory.

Discouragement's mission is to disarm the courage within us. Let me say that again. The purpose of discouragement is to disarm our courage. And what is the purpose of courage? It takes courage to step through our doorways of destiny and to fulfill God's mandate on our lives. Basically, discouragement is a thief trying to break into our house of identity and rob us of our current and future destiny. Discouragement sets out to steal our God-breathed destiny.

We are called to walk in great courage, to encourage ourselves and those around us. Finding keys to courage that work in our lives is monumental to great victories for us and others. We are to be a people that lift up others in courage to fulfill their God-given dreams and destiny. We need courage to bring heaven to earth. These keys are to help strengthen us in courage, so we can encourage and strengthen others.

1. REMEMBERING WHO YOU ARE

"I can't afford to have a thought in my head about myself that isn't in His." – Bill Johnson

Reminding ourselves that we our God's loved, approved and accepted sons and daughters apart from anything we do takes the performance pressure off! When we can rest and bask in His unconditional love for us, it sets us free to love others. When I start feeling afraid of stepping out, I remind myself of how much I am loved and accepted no matter what happens. I say to myself, "Jason, you are the most loved son and nothing can take that away from you. Boy, are you loved and accepted!" I will usually feel God's pleasure and the Holy Spirit's presence as I focus on His love for me. As I focus on God's presence, that increases too. The more I focus on enjoying Him, fear lessens.

I remind myself of who God says I am through the prophetic words that I have received. If you do not have any prophetic words for your life, then look into a mirror and give yourself some using the training from the last chapter. Also record what God says about you are in His Word. The Bible is full of scriptures on our identity. Bill Johnson carries a stack of 4X6 cards with his prophetic words written on them everywhere he goes to make sure his thoughts about himself line up with God's thoughts. I have personally recorded all the main prophecies over my life and put them to soaking music on my iPod. If I feel disconnected from courage, I listen to my prophetic words and pretty soon I recognize the voice of my Father and say to the accuser of discouragement, "Liar, that is not who I am...My Father says this about me!" Our heart is a garden and it is up to us to cultivate and keep it clear of weeds of lies. We need to continually soak our heart with the living water of His truth about our identity. Repetitively remind yourself of who God says you are in His written Word and with your personal prophetic words. This is a powerful and important lifestyle to a sustaining walk of courage. You are a mighty, fearless, valiant warrior called to do great exploits with King Jesus!

2. Taking That First Step

"Faith is taking the first step even when you don't see the whole staircase." – Martin Luther King, Jr.

In Joshua Chapter 3, the Lord tells Joshua to have the priests carry the Ark of His promise to the Jordan River's edge. The Lord says that when they step into the water, the Jordan River will part and the children of Israel will walk across on dry land. The water did not part as the priests stood by the edge looking into the water.

> *Yet as soon as the priests who carried the ark reached the Jordan and their feet touched the water's edge, the water from upstream stopped flowing. It piled up in a heap a great distance away, at a town called Adam in the vicinity of Zarethan, while the water flowing down to the Sea of the Arabah (that is, the Dead Sea) was completely cut off. So the people crossed over opposite Jericho...on dry ground"* (Joshua 3:14-17)

The power of God was released the moment that they stepped into the water. This is another major supernatural kingdom principle. God's grace is released the moment we step into the impossible situation. God usually won't move until after we take the first step. The miracle is released as we put ourselves in a position to confront the impossible. The grace and supernatural power isn't released while standing on the river's bank. We must take that first big step and get our feet wet.

I have been pursuing a lifestyle to step out in power in public to release God's love for about four years now. I have stepped out thousands of times now and the first approach on the first encounter of the day still feels the most intimidating and awkward. I may feel nervous even when the situation does not appear as hostile as my last story. It could be a group of well-mannered teenagers or a school teacher, and yet the first step on the first encounter is still the hardest for me. I still chicken out sometimes and prod myself saying, "Jason, did you really just chicken out?" I will then dust myself off and go swing the bat again at another ball. We cannot stop this thing! Too many people need Him who lives inside of us. They desperately need Jesus! The world without Jesus is drowning, and it's up to us to throw them life jackets.

When I was serving tables at Olive Garden, the first table of my shift was always the same. I always seemed to fumble through the introduction on my first table. I felt so clumsy and awkward. I would be acutely aware of every word that came out of my mouth. I would be thinking to myself, "You're talking way too fast...slow down...smile...Jason, relax...pretend they are friends that are at your house for dinner." I would have to coach my way through the first table each night. In fact, one time during my first table, I accidentally introduced myself as my roommate. I said, "Hello, thanks for joining us tonight. My name is Mark." The guest said, "But your name tag reads Jason." After the third and fourth table of the night, I would start to sail. I would quit thinking about my introduction lines and get in the groove. I would loosen up and really start enjoying the guests, because the focus was off me now and on them. The night would fly by and I would have lots of fun.

179

It is similar to this for me when praying for people in public. The first approach usually feels a little weird and awkward. Even asking them to pray on the first encounter feels a little uncomfortable. A lot of times, I will use the basic prayer model with my first person because I feel more comfortable with it to start with. But as soon as I begin to pray or prophesy over that first person, the Holy Spirit currents seem to start flowing and I am able to focus more on them than on me. The next encounter, even if in the same group but to the next person, is easier because Holy Spirit momentum is going. Then the next group is easier and miracles start happening and pretty soon we are open air preaching and calling out words of knowledge and a revival riot is in full-blown motion. The kingdom of God is now popping like popcorn all around us. People are encountering Jesus through miracles signs and wonders. Souls are being saved and healed! I go home that night and think, "This is why we were created, to kill giants!"

The next day we go out and I think that we will continue from where we left off as far as courage goes, but it feels like I'm starting all over again. It is easier, but there is still resistance when I first get going. It takes courage again to take that first step. Usually the first step on my first encounter is the biggest breakthrough in courage of that day. Where I am in boldness now to where I was three years ago is a night and day difference. I am not the same person. Thank You, Jesus.

3. WHEN LOVE FLOWS FEAR GOES

Try this exercise: Look at an object on the wall to your left. Focus on it. Now look at an object on the wall on your right. Focus on it. Now focus on both objects at the same time. Ha, you can't do it! It's virtually impossible to simultaneously focus on two opposing objects at the same time. In the same way, it is impossible for you to focus on your own fear and on God's love. Love and fear are polar opposites and you cannot focus on them both at the same time. You will either be in love or in fear. It depends on where your focus is.

Dr. Caroline Leaf in her book, *The Gift Within You*, says that every type of emotion has one of only two roots: Love or fear. Scientists have researched the anatomy and physiology of love and fear right down to a molecular, genetic and epigenetic level. They found a deeper system in the brain concerned with positive love emotions and negative fear emotions. Scientists have discovered that fear and love cannot coexist in any one conscious moment. We operate in one or the other depending on the thoughts we think. Science shows that there is a massive flushing of negative toxic thoughts when we operate in love. The brain releases a chemical that literally melts away negative toxic thought clusters.[1] Loves literally wipes out fear!

> *"There is no fear in love [dread does not exist], but full-grown (complete, perfect) love turns fear out of doors and expels every trace of terror!..."* (1 John 4:18 Amplified Bible).

At BSSM, there was a girl that our entire school looked up to for her boldness and fearless love for others. On my first ministry trip, I asked her, "How are you so bold in public when you minister to others?" Her response really helped me a lot. She said, "When I feel fear and insecurity, I realize it is self-focused. So, I ask the Lord to give me His love for the person in front of me. I ask Him, 'What do you love about this person?' I am focusing all of my attention outward on God's love for them. The more I am able to partner with

God's love toward that person, the less I notice fear and insecurity."

God's love is like a river that flows from God's throne into me. Then that river flows out of me to touch others. When I feel fear in loving others, I focus my attention on receiving God's unconditional love for me. Then, I allow that perfect love to flow out of me to others. Take that first step of being focused outward in love. When love flows, fear goes.

4. Revival is Risky Business

"Faith is spelled R-I-S-K." – John Wimber

At Bethel Church, we endorse John Wimber's famed quote, "Faith is spelled R-I-S-K." It announces that God is pleased with our risk-taking more than in the outcome that the risk produced. I first saw this modeled well at BSSM when the students were given an opportunity to share testimonies of what they had seen God do on our outreach. A young lady went up and shared a story of someone being healed out of a wheelchair in Wal-Mart. We all jumped to our feet, loudly cheering and exuberantly celebrating the miraculous healing that Jesus had done through her.

Then the instructor asked someone to share a testimony where nothing seemingly happened, but they had taken a risk to step out to love someone. A young male student slowly raised his hand. Uncomfortably he shared his testimony of failure and non-achievement. He said that he had prayed for his first physical healing in Safeway. He had prayed for a man's knee but nothing had happened. Out of pity, our entire class quietly golf-clapped. I personally remember feeling, "Bummer for you. Better luck next time."

What transpired in the next few minutes changed my life. Our entire class was about to receive a huge paradigm shift. The instructor took this opportunity to share how both testimonies took an equal amount of risk and courage. He said that God had been just as pleased with the second testimony as He was with the first one. He shared how we can often be too results-oriented. God looks at our heart to love others and He is so pleased whenever we step out in risk to love someone regardless of what we believe the results were.

The instructor went on to say that our part is to take the risk to step out and God's part is the rest. He said that many great history-making exploits started with a great risk. The risk-taker is the catalyst that releases God's kingdom. He encouraged us to jump up, yell and cheer just as loud for the second testimony of risk as we did for the wheelchair miracle, because both students took a great risk. Our entire class jumped up and cheered and celebrated the young man for his risk-taking, aside from any results. As we did this, I felt something break off our class and a true freedom was released for us to take risks.

PRAYER: *"I pray right now that all fear of performance will break off your life and you will be free to take great risks to love others apart from results. I pray that you will be a radical risk-taker of love, reaching lives around you everywhere you go. I release supernatural courage and destiny over you now in Jesus' name! Holy Spirit, I ask you tangibly rest upon each one now with a great measure."*

RISK-DARES

During my Second Year of BSSM, I had the idea that it would be fun to have a risk buddy to challenge each other's risk levels as we went out to love on people. I had already been stepping out, but I knew there was more. I thought it would be a good idea to dare each other to take bigger supernatural risks.

We would go out together to love on people in public. If we saw a group of people, we may challenge each other to a dare like this: "I dare you to go up that group and prophesy over one person and get two words of knowledge for healing. I dare you to heal that person with your shadow." (Ha ha, I got so excited just now that I ran downstairs and told my roommate that we should go out and do risk- dares tomorrow.)

These risk-dares help me keep the fun factor alive in the supernatural. Other risk-dares have been: "I dare you to get three specific words of knowledge about one healing for the next person we meet." An example would be healing for a left ankle: that was from a sports injury (w.o.k. #1), it happened five years ago (w.o.k. #2), and their pain level is at a 7 (w.o.k. #3). Doing risk-dares like this helps us stretch our current supernatural muscles. It helps us push the comfort-zone boundaries in our lives out a little farther. It is also really fun.

Incorporate some sort of risk-dare into your life for fun. Your first dare may be: I dare you to smile at a stranger and say, "Jesus loves you! Do you need a hug?"

5. Change your what ifs

A couple of years ago the Holy Spirit said, "I want you to change your *what ifs*. He said, "Instead of saying, 'What if that person in the wheelchair is not healed,' instead say, 'What if that person in that wheelchair is healed! How would that affect her life? Wow, what if that happened right now!" Pay attention to your self-talk and practice changing your negative what ifs. Start dreaming of crazy awesome what ifs. God said He wants to do more than we can think or imagine…Wow, what if!

6. Practicing to Learn

My friend, Caleb, shared an insight with me that has helped with my personal courage level. He said "When we go out to pray for people we should embrace the attitude that we are practicing to learn how to love people." If our objective is in learning, it will never be about success or failure. It is all about us partnering with the Holy Spirit and learning from Him. If our heart is to learn to love others, it helps us avoid a performance mentality.

My dad was a professionally ranked tennis player in the 1970's and 1980's, so by default I grew up playing on the tennis courts. Years ago I played tennis competitively. During tournaments while warming up for a match, my strokes were smooth and relaxed. I had seamless long sweeping groundstrokes. At the start of the match, my swings remained smooth and effortless. However, during the match if I started thinking too much about the score or how much I needed to win the next few points, I would tense up. If I began self-talking about not hitting the net or not hitting it long, my swing would change. My smooth sweeping strokes morphed into short, choppy, defensive strokes. I would deliberately tell myself to relax, loosen up and just swing and hit the ball. Sometimes in order to relax, I pretended I was still warming up, just practicing my groundstrokes.

In the same way, I have also noticed that if I'm praying for the sick and think too much about what will happen or won't happen, I tense up. It helps going out with the attitude that I am practicing to learn, because really the more I can get out of the way the more the kingdom comes. When I start to feel the pressure to perform, I take a big gulp of God's presence and realize again that I am a student of the Holy Spirit. I remember "He is healing." I invite Him to come in a greater measure. When He comes good things happen.

7. Sowing Seeds of Love

In the Biblical days of farming, seeds were thrown onto an unplowed field. The farmer would then locate the seeds lying on top of the soil, and that would be where he would run his plow.

Our main job in a supernatural lifestyle is to throw "love seed" on people's lives. Whenever we share the love of Jesus with someone, we are throwing seed on their lives. Whether or not they seem open to it at that point, that is irrelevant. The seed is already on them, meaning the Father is soon to follow with the plow! They are now marked by heaven for another God encounter. They have a great big giant neon bull's eye on the top of their head marked for heaven. Heaven's GPS system won't miss this target!

When someone rejects me as I'm sharing Jesus with them, I tell them, "No worries", but inwardly I'm smiling and saying to myself, "It's too late. You have seed on you now! The plow is on its way!"

A quick note about rejection. A friend, Todd White, says this. "If you are accepted in Christ, then it is impossible for someone to reject you. You are accepted not rejected." It is true people can and will reject us as we share Jesus. Jesus Himself was rejected. But our identity in being accepted by the Father triumphs any rejection. Our identity is rock solid in being affirmed, loved and accepted in Him apart from anything we can do for Him. This makes us free to love others. Allow the truth of your identity to possess you.

God doesn't give up on people. He is really good at wearing down the hardest heart with His unfailing love. The hardest materials in the world can be eroded away by a continual dripping of water. The hardest heart is no match for God's continual dripping of unconditional love. God just asks that we give His love away.

For weeks a certain teenager mocked my friends at local high school football games. He called them many profane names week after week. My friends were there at the games ministering to the youth. Even though this young man would say the vilest things to my friends, they kept their love toward this young man. They continued telling him how awesome he was, and they kept prophesying destiny and goodness over his life. This young man continued to harass them week after week, but they kept loving him just the same. Toward the end of the season, this young man started to open his heart up to my friends and eventually asked Jesus to be his Lord and Savior. He was obviously very hurt in life and God's persistent love softened his hardened heart. He ended up becoming a huge catalyst for Jesus at the last few football games. He became the great evangelist, going out and bringing all the kids over to witness the good news of his new Lord, Savior and Friend!

8. TRUSTING IN GOD'S LOVE AND HIS ABILITY

I have grown to trust in God's ability way beyond mine. I have come to the revelation that He loves people way more than I do, and He knows what He is doing even if I am clueless. He can heal despite any doubt or unbelief that is present within me or the person I am ministering to. I focus on His ability, on His love and on His anointing, not mine. My words of knowledge fail and my love lessens, but His never does. God is not limited by my lack of gifting or anointing. I just give Him the opportunity to show up by taking risks. I realize that the Holy Spirit is with me. I focus on His presence, and then I step into a situation trusting that God is God and I am not. I put my hope and trust in the fact that He is good and He really loves people and wants to help them. My part is to step into the river of impossibility with the Ark of His presence, the great Holy Spirit. When I do, I trust in His love for others. God asks us to do the impossible. There is no security in what God asks us to do. There is only security in who God is.

Joaquin Evans, at his healing schools, often opens the first meeting saying this, "I do not know how to heal anybody. The only problem with that is everything in my job description has something to do with healing. My job is to heal the sick, and I do not know how to do it. I am just glad that my best friend the Holy Spirit does, and He is really good at His job!" It's all about making a place of intimacy with the Holy Spirit and His presence and then trusting Him with the results.

We just choose to love extravagantly, throwing love seeds everywhere we go, and trust God to run the plow. We don't always get to see the results. We need to put the results in God's hands. Outwardly a situation could look like the greatest failure, but we don't know what's happening inside people's hearts. We can only control what we do and that is to reach out and love people.

My friend Tara shared this personal life story with me. Tara and a bunch of her high school friends were on a beach in Southern California, having a bonfire beach party. They were mostly high school students out on summer break. They were drinking beer and hard alcohol. A young man approached the students and started to tell them about Jesus. The entire group turned on this young man and practically mobbed him. They threw beer bottles at him, spit on him and called him the most hideous names. As the group continued to mock him, he quietly disappeared into the darkness. This young man saw nothing good happen from his efforts to share God's love. It appeared in the natural as a massive failure and a great defeat.

What he didn't know was that my friend who was there was so impacted and cut to the heart. In that moment she ran home crying, went upstairs to her bedroom, shut the door, got on her knees and asked Jesus back into her heart. She had been a back-slidden Christian for years and the boldness and love of that young man pierced her soul. She was set on fire with the love of Jesus that night in her room and has been radically following Him ever since. I heard her story in BSSM. She now travels the world to share God's love with others. God has used her powerfully to minister to thousands, seeing many healed and saved. This young man that was so influential in her life has no idea of the fruit that awaits him someday in heaven. All he saw the night at the beach was brutal rejection.

Mahesh Chavda is an evangelist that currently has seen around 700,000 people come to Jesus through his ministry. When Mahesh was an 8 year-old Hindu boy, he was given a small New Testament Bible from a lady missionary in exchange for a cold cup of water. He kept reading his Bible and praying to God asking Him if this was the truth. Jesus ended up appearing to him in a vision and revealing to Him who He was. God has used Mahesh's life to radically affect this generation with the Gospel of Jesus. He has never again seen the missionary who gave him that New Testament in exchange for that cup of cold water. Her life has impacted hundreds of thousands for Jesus through one simple act of love.

Mr. Genor on George Street

There was a traveling Baptist minister who visited many different countries on a world tour. In every place he visited, he took the head minister to lunch and asked them how they personally received Jesus. Shockingly, many of these ministers had the exact same story of personal salvation. Although the years of their conversion varied, each one had this same amazing story: "I was visiting Australia and ended up on George Street. A little, white-haired man stepped out in front of me, offered me a pamphlet and said, 'Excuse me, are you saved? If you died tonight, would you go to heaven?' This bothered me so much that I searched out a minister and shortly thereafter gave my life to Jesus."

This Baptist minister was so shocked that all of these ministers, head chaplains and missionaries from around the world were similarly saved--through a track given to them by this little white-haired man on George St. in Australia. This Baptist minister was scheduled for a trip to Australia and he made a point to search out who this mysterious little, white-haired man was. The Baptist minister asked the local parish if they had heard of him. They said, "Oh yes, that is Mr. Genor, but he is too old and frail now to give out tracts. He lives in an apartment down by George Street. Would you like to visit him?"

The Baptist minister visited Mr. Genor and shared the accounts of these leaders all over the world that were saved by a white-haired man on George Street giving them a tract. Mr. Genor started to tremble and tears came to his eyes as he shared, "I was so overwhelmed with the love of God that after I retired, I tried to give away ten tracts a day down on George Street. I have given those tracts away for over twenty years now. This is the first I have heard anything about those tracts."[2] Mr. Genor died two weeks later. Mr. Genor said he was simply compelled by love for his Savior.

We can't measure the results of our lives by what we see or don't see. In heaven some day we will see it all. I'm sure we will be truly amazed, seeing that God did extravagant things with our smallest acts of love and kindness.

MY LANDLORD'S NIECE

I went to pay my rent and Angela my landlord asked me, "Were you at the mall last Saturday between six and eight in the evening? Did you pray for a girl with a crutch in the Verizon store?" I said to her, "Nope, that wasn't me. Why? What happened?" She continued, "Well, it was my niece that was prayed for in the mall. When she was a young girl, she broke her leg and her growth plate was damaged. Because of the damage, her right leg was about one inch shorter then her left one. She has had to have special shoes with a one inch thicker sole on her right shoe to make up the difference."

Angela continued telling me the story: "She was in the mall last Saturday looking at a new phone and two people approached her asking why she had to have a crutch. She told them about her shorter leg, so they asked if they could pray for her. They prayed several times for her leg to grow out, but nothing happened. My niece woke up the next day and when she got out of bed and started to walk around, she noticed that something felt very different. She yelled, 'Mom, come here. I think my leg grew last night!'

When my sister measured my niece's legs, her right leg had grown out! God must have lengthened her leg while she was sleeping. They got dressed right away and went to the store to buy my niece a pair of even-soled shoes. She hadn't been able to wear even-soled shoes since she was a little girl. My niece wore her brand new normal shoes to church that day. My whole family has never believed in miracles, and now they can't quit telling everyone what God did!"

Later that night, I was sharing this testimony at Campus Awakening youth. My friend, Dane, perked up in his chair and exclaimed, "That was me! That was me and Vanessa Burkhart. We prayed for her! Are you kidding me, her leg really grew out? We left the mall disappointed because we thought nothing had happened to her. That is so awesome!" We do not always get to see the results of our love.

LET'S PLAN SOME RISK TAKING GOALS

As with all the things in life that are important to us and to God, it is a good idea to plan for success. If you plan on getting married someday, you should think about what you need to do to be ready for marriage. Maybe you should start wearing underarm deodorant or upgrade your wardrobe. Expectant mothers make preparations for a newborn child. They make plans on where the baby will sleep and they buy a crib. When going to war, an army makes strategic plans for victory. In the same way, in our personal walk with Jesus and when pursuing a revival lifestyle, we must make a plan for success. One of the greatest ways that the Lord has helped me to sustain a thriving relationship with Him and a lifestyle of the supernatural is to strategically make goals for my life.

Mr. Genor on George Street had a practical plan to give away ten tracts a day. Those goals helped him fulfill his destiny to reach the lost. He didn't know of any results for over twenty years, but look at what God did through his life of consistency and faithfulness in reaching out to share Jesus. When I was in my first year at BSSM, I started making goals to take more risks. It would look something like this: Pray for one person a day for healing and prophesy over one person a day. I would keep track of my risk-goals and check them off each day. This was a great way for me to stay focused on living a revival lifestyle.

Goal setting is a great way to stay focused on a target. If you desire to heal the sick, you will have to pray for the sick. If you desire to walk in miracle-working power, you will need to pray for people that need a miracle. Most of the time, it is inconvenient to stop and pray for people in public. We are always on our way somewhere to see somebody. I have noticed that making daily goals to pray for people helps me to be more aware of the people around me that need Jesus. It helps me take off the blinders, so to speak. When I'm in Wal-Mart just buying laundry soap and the lady standing next to me looks depressed, if I have a risk-goal to make three people's day a little happier, then I am more apt to stop and take a few minutes to love and encourage her.

Having daily goals to impact others lives with the love and power of Jesus is a great way to plan for revival success. If you are not intentional about growing in risk-taking, you will never grow beyond your last level. We grow our spiritual muscles by pushing against greater resistance. Just like body builders must increase the resistance or weight they lift to keep growing, we must push against greater levels of resistance too. I encourage you to make some risk-goals for this week to step out past your comfort zone and to release Jesus on the people around you.

Yesterday, I realized I needed to prophesy over one more person to reach my daily goal, and I was in the McDonald's drive-thru around 10 p.m. I got to speak a word of encouragement to the lady working the drive-thru window. Her entire countenance lifted as she embraced the fact that God really does love her and has a great plan for her life. She said, "Thank you! You have no idea how much I needed to hear that!" The gospel isn't complicated, but it may seem inconvenient in our busy schedule. That is why I encourage you to make a plan to intentionally release God's goodness using risk-goals.

My risk-goal today was to pray for three people's healing and to prophesy over three strangers going about my normal day. I got to see five miracles of healing and prophesied over seven people.

Like most people, I am busy with life's demands. At the writing of this chapter, I am a single dad with kids at home and work a secular job. I oversee a branch of the Supernatural Outreach Department at Bethel and do supernatural conferences that keep me occupied. It is easy for me to get in a routine of scheduled ministry, only praying for people on specified outreach times each week. That is not the model Jesus set for us. He did life and released heaven as he went. We are heaven's resource to people. Again I challenge you like I challenge myself to make a plan for revival success in your life daily. Set specific risk-goals for yourself, asking the Holy Spirit what that looks like, and then go for it!

Here is a list of risk goals from our incredible youth at Campus Awakening in Redding. Each * represents a different high school student.

* Tell someone that Jesus loves them.

* Pray for a friend who is not a Christian, who is feeling sad or depressed.

* Pray for one healing a day and prophesy over one stranger.

* Pray for the guy with the cast and prophesy over three people.

* Heal somebody with my shadow.

* Pray three times for someone this week.

* Tell one person that God loves them each day this week.

* Prophesy over two people.

* Give two words of knowledge outside the church each day.

* Pray for two people a day, prophecy over someone everyday and pray for the paralytic person at my school.

Activation: Ask the Holy Spirit to give you some risk-goals for this week. It may be to just strike up a conversation with a stranger. It may be to smile at someone and say, "Have a nice day." Maybe you will prophesy or pray for someone's healing. Just ask the Holy Spirit what would be a stretch for you this week. You can do this! This is what you were born for, to change the world with King Jesus!

ENDNOTES

1. *The Gift Within You* by Dr. Caroline Leaf (South Lake, TX: Thomas Nelson Publications, 2009), pg 143.

2. Mr. Genor, http://www.freecdtracts.com/testimony_11.htm

 **ACTION STEP**

• Watch Video #9 - Mr. Genor's Story

• Write out some R.I.S.K. goals

Chapter 10

Normal Marketplace Ministry

"Don't go for their jugular, go for their heart." -Todd White

These are some simple basic guidelines to help you minister to others in the marketplace. Love and honor should be the foundation from where we minister. When we are ministering to someone, we need to always keep this in mind: "What is the best way to love and honor this person or this business that I am in right now?" Love and honor should be at the forefront of our heart in every situation.

I am sharing some general core values and basics that have helped me minister in public settings. Every single encounter will be different so learn to trust in the Holy Spirit's ability to guide you. The Holy Spirit in you is big enough for every situation. He is a big God!

Did You Learn to Love?

"We are not born with love; we get to learn how to love." – Bob Jones

Prophet Bob Jones was taken to heaven. When he was in line waiting to get into heaven, he saw that Jesus was asking each person just one question. That was it, one question, the same question to each person.

This was the one question Jesus asked everyone..."Did you learn to love?"

People are not projects. We need to make sure that we are not going out to try to fix someone else. We are here to love and honor people, even with their differences. My mode of ministry is: "If I can just make one person's life a little brighter today, then that's ministry." If I am going out to see a miracle, I could be disappointed. But if my motive is to love someone, I can never be wrong.

People are smart; they can sniff out our hidden agendas and motives. Have you ever test-driven a car from a cheesy, used car dealership? The larger than life used car salesman may smile and say something like, "Howdy, I'm cowboy Roy and I am here for you guys. My job is to make sure you get a sweeeeet deal and that you are one hundred percent satissssfied" Reaching down, you make sure that your wallet is still safe by your side, because although he is saying all the right words, you aren't feeling the love. People can tell if we aren't really there to help them. They can detect our hidden agendas.

Todd White says it best, "Don't go for their jugular, go for their heart." If we are being motivated by trying to reach our miracle quota for the month over trying to love well, we may end up doing some collateral damage. If I want to get one more salvation testimony so I can feel good about myself, how's that working out for me? Heart motives are important. Why do we want to move in power? Is it to help others? These are important questions.

During Second Year at BSSM, the Lord had me stop ministering to others for forty days, because I was starting to get my identity based on the miracles I was seeing on the streets. If I saw Jesus do great miracles through me, I felt anointed, awesome and loved that day. If I prayed for people the next day and I saw nothing happen, I didn't feel as good about myself as I did the day before. The Lord had me stop ministering to others for a season so that He could re-align my identity in Him as being His son that He loves and is pleased with apart from anything I do. While ministering to others, I talk to myself saying things like, "Jason, don't go for their jugular, go for their heart. Papa, show me their heart. Fill me with your love for them. I want to see them through your eyes."

God's love is compelling and relentless. As we allow His love for others to consume us and compel us, then we really can't be rejected. If our only motive is to love, we can't be shut down. They may say, "No thanks," but we look them in the eye, smile full of God's acceptance, and say, "That's okay, brother. You are awesome and Jesus loves you and has a great plan for your life. I bless you." Love never fails! Honestly, we don't even need this book or any other if we can just be completely possessed by love itself. Love will go the distance. It sees no failure. Heidi Baker says, "Love looks like something. It looks like food to the hungry. It looks like a smile and hug to the lonely. It looks like a blanket to the one that is cold. It looks like a miracle of healing to the sick."

We are to be love incarnate to the world around us. Jesus loves the world and died for each and every person on this planet. Love looks like stopping for someone, smiling and looking into his or her eyes, and giving love away towards their need. Love is making another's day better and brighter.

A few months back we were filming some Jesus miracles in the marketplace. We were trying to get words of knowledge for healing the sick. The whole morning felt pretty dull and disconnected. We had ministered healing prayer to a few people, but hadn't seen many results. I was pondering what was going wrong. I thought to myself, "Why does today seem off?" We pulled toward the exit of a parking lot, and I noticed an elderly lady holding a sign for money. I didn't have any cash with me, but as we pulled up I felt a flood of love for this lady. I jumped out of the car and said, "I don't have any money, but can I give you a hug?" Her eyes brightened and I gave her the biggest hug. I felt like I was hugging my own grandmother. I said, "Jesus and I love you" and jumped back into the car. Suddenly, everything felt "right" again. My focus was off seeing miracles and back onto love. My heart was repositioned on love. The grateful smile and glow in that grandma's eyes after giving her a hug was what love looked like in that moment to this little precious lady. Jesus wants to destroy the works of the devil through us, but our focus must be on loving people not fixing projects or getting a good testimony. God loves people.

Marketplace Basic Training

Here are some practical basics of marketplace ministry that I have learned. These are not formulas, but, like training wheels, they may help you get started. Use these with the basic training you received in Chapter 8 for healing the sick and prophecy. Once you are on your way, I pray that the Holy Spirit gives you many insights into loving others in power. When He does I hope that you will write a book to help others and me.

The Approach

The approach is all about making people feel comfortable and safe. Do not have large groups approach smaller ones. That would be overwhelming for them. The same number of people should match or be smaller than the number of people that you are approaching. Also, try to approach people of the same gender as you have in your group if possible. This is for obvious practical reasons, but again listen to Holy Spirit.

The Introduction

"Let us always meet each other with a smile, for the smile is the beginning of love." – Mother Theresa

Be sincere. Be yourself! If you are nervous it's okay to say, "I am a little nervous doing this because this is new for me. I really just felt in my heart that I was suppose to come up and talk to you....I felt like God wanted you to know how special you are and...." Be sincere. It is way better to be real and honest rather than trying to memorize a script like a robot. People respond well to genuineness. They will most likely be very happy that someone took time to try to love them today.

Don't try to be spiritual or anointed. Be yourself! Be the same you as when you are talking to a small group of your friends. Be sensitive to any time constraints they may have. Remember this encounter is to bless them. The person standing in front of us is the reason we are there. Be love.

Be conscious and intentional to not to use churchy lingo. In our church subculture, we have created our own language, *Christianese*. The un-churched do not understand this foreign language. I witnessed a prophetic person say this while ministering to a teenager at In and Out Burger, "Glory, brother! I see the anointing running from the top of your head down your garments like a royal diadem! Just like on Aaron's garments, the glory is all over you, man! You have a prophetic mantle inside of you, shaba!" The young man's facial expression of mass confusion got more contorted with each passing phrase. When speaking in the marketplace avoid abstract words. Keep it simple. Use communication that they will understand. A good way to gauge this is to use the same natural language you would in your secular workplace.

Praying in Public

"Love the one in front of you." -Heidi Baker

When praying for people in public, it's important to ask permission to put our hand on someone to pray for them. Have girls pray for girls and guys pray for guys when possible. Use common sense when applying your hands. If the pain is on a girl's stomach, have her put her hand over where it hurts. If you are a girl, you could place your hand over hers. If you are a guy, touch her shoulder with permission. Holy Spirit doesn't need us to touch them. Make sure that the person you are ministering to feels safe, honored and protected. If your hand shakes when you pray, don't lay hands on them; just release God's presence over them. Try to practice praying with your eyes open when ministering in public. Please do not shout or pray in tongues when you pray for people in the marketplace. People do not have a grid for that.

ASKING TO PRAY

This is one of the greatest things that has helped me make others feel comfortable to receive prayer in public. Rarely do I ask questions like, "Is it okay if we pray for you?" Instead I will say, "Let us pray for you," as I reach my hand outward towards theirs.

What is the difference you may say?

Asking "Is it okay if we pray for you?" requires them to answer with a yes or no response. They are wondering what will happen if they say yes or no. Many times out of politeness or uncertainty people will say "No, thanks," thinking they are doing us a favor. When you say, "Let us pray for you," as you extend your hand toward theirs, they feel comfortable. You are communicating that you know what you are doing, and they will grab your hand for prayer. At this point, I just release healing, "Be healed; pain, go," and then ask them "Test it out." Many times they are healed before they realize what has just happened to them. I have noticed the fewer questions we ask that require a yes or no response from them, the more comfortable they are.

After I find out what their prayer need is, I will say, "Do me a favor and grab my hand," or "Do me a favor and come sit in this chair. I believe one of your legs is shorter." We are there to help them and we can. Ask fewer questions and help lead them into their healing. They are giving me permission to heal them when they grab my hand or when they sit in the chair.

Another good way to minister healing is to ask, "Where exactly is the pain?" When they touch the point of pain, (Let's say it's on their elbow) I will say, "Keep your hand right there. I am going to pray for you." Then I release healing and have them test it out.

What if they say, "No thank you"?

If they say no, that is okay. Again, do not take it personally. It is not our job to unlock hearts. It is the Holy Spirit's job. If they say no, I will usually try to give them an encouraging prophetic word, unless I sense that they are in a time constraint. I want them to feel loved and honored through this encounter no matter what happens. I may press in again, asking to pray for the healing if I sense they have opened up more. I really believe we have the answer to help them in whatever they need. If someone has had constant back pain for fifteen years, five minutes of their time to be healed is not much of an inconvenience. They will thank us for being persistent after they are healed.

We want to be confident in love but not pushy or pesky. We have Jesus, the answer to their need, but not everyone will see the value in Him or in us. If they do not want anything from us, I will smile and say, "Okay, bless you" and go to the next person. Remember we cannot be rejected if we are already accepted in Jesus. Focus on His love and acceptance for you. Be aware of His presence and make sure to have lots of fun! The Holy Spirit will have other open doors ready for us as we keep going to love people.

What if the pain moves around when you pray?

That usually means it is a demonic spirit of infirmity. Do not tell the person that they have a demon called infirmity. That may scare them. They do not need to hear that the pain is linked to a demonic spirit in order to get free. Again, use wisdom. We do not want to create fear in the person we are ministering to. If the pain increases or moves during prayer, that is an indication that it is usually a spirit. You do not need to call it a spirit out loud during prayer.

A spirit is named after the persona they possess. A spirit of anger manifests anger. A spirit of poverty brings poverty. You do not need to address me, "Human Jason." I know I am a human, just like a spirit knows it is a spirit. I wouldn't need to tell the person, "I discovered that you have a spirit of infirmity." I would just say, "It's an infirmity, and we are going to get it out of your body now." In my heart I know that I am casting out a spirit and I calmly and firmly command, "Infirmity, come out." Then I ask them what they are sensing. The spirit will leave. Sometimes you may need to pray a few times, but it will go. *But if I drive out demons by the finger of God, then the kingdom of God has come to you* (Luke 11:20). I enjoy casting out devils because doing so helps people and displays that Jesus is King and Lord!

Holy Spirit Presence Encounter

Depending on the situation and if there is time, I will try to bring the person I'm ministering to into a personal God encounter. A miracle or prophetic word will unlock their hearts, but we will be gone in a minute. My desire is to get them connected to the Source for themselves. I may have them hold out their hands and invite the Holy Spirit to come and then have them become aware of His presence. I will ask what they are experiencing. I will have them close their eyes and see if God shows them anything. I will have them ask Jesus, "What do you love about me?" and then ask them what they are sensing. I am helping them get supernaturally connected to God for themselves. I encourage them to continue to pursue this very real and personal God on their own. I say things like, "You can experience God like this anytime you want. When you go home tonight start talking to Him."

SALVATION-THE GREATEST MIRACLE

"We are to plunder hell to populate heaven for Calvary's sake...We are not threatening people with hell, we are warning them. You threaten an enemy. You warn those you love"– Reinhard Bonnke

Share the Gospel of salvation. Share Jesus! It's great to ask people if they have a real personal thriving relationship with Jesus. I ask people, "Are you born again?" Reinhard Bonnke said, "What good is it to heal a cripple if they can now walk straight to hell without a limp?" God is after eternal salvation for the entire world! One of the greatest privileges and mandates on our lives is to share the Gospel of salvation.

If someone is healed, share how Jesus came not only to take sickness and sin from them, He came to have a relationship with them. Explain the Gospel and how Jesus was born to a virgin, was crucified, and rose the third day. Explain how they need a Savior because of sin, and they can be born again today. Ask if they want to be saved and adopted into God's family. My heart burns for people to meet and fall in love with Jesus. People coming to Jesus and getting saved for eternity is the greatest miracle of all. It will forever be the greatest mission and mandate. One person getting saved is worth more than many lifetimes of other pursuits.

In our passion for the lost, we need to make sure that we do not begin to love souls more than people. We cannot view people as mere numbers or salvation notches on our heavenly belts. Our goal is not to have people repeat a prayer after us. A repeated prayer does not save, but faith in Jesus Christ does. A salvation prayer model is good. I use them but unless it is mixed with faith in their heart, it is just a recital. My mission is to connect them to Jesus Himself! We not only want to get them saved from something (hell), but saved into something (the kingdom of God)!

The Gospel is always relevant, in every country in every generation. It is the Good News. Reinhard Bonnke says, "We do not threaten people with the Gospel; we warn them. You threaten an enemy. You warn those that you care about".

Last year in prayer the Lord showed me a vision of missing children's pictures on milk cartons. He said, "Son, these are all my lost and missing children." I believe God let me feel for a brief moment a taste of the incredible pain that a parent of a missing child must carry. I started to travail in the Spirit over these missing kids. I felt an agonizing pain and the grief of a parent with a missing child. I screamed and sobbed uncontrollably in the Spirit. I felt God say that He feels this great pain, loss and torment too. Each person that does not know Him or is not living safe in the Father's house is His missing child. I felt He was asking me with a desperation and pain, "Jason, go find my missing children and bring them home to safety, love and security in My house. Go and find them; bring them home before it's too late for them...please!"

God really loves each person so intimately. He is not aloof or distant even with those that He knows will ultimately reject Him. He does not guard His heart from pain because of fear of being hurt. God's heart is crushed with every person that dies and goes to hell. You cannot convince me otherwise. Jesus paid such a tortuous death for the love of His lost children. God's greatest mission was Jesus coming to rescue them.

> "For God so loved the world that he gave his one and
> only Son, that whoever believes in him shall not perish
> but have eternal life" (John 3:16).

His missing children have been kidnapped and abducted by a deceptive world system and dragged into believing its lies. It is our mission to rescue them and bring them home to their loving Father, so they too can begin to enjoy real life in the Father's house.

All of heaven rejoices over one sinner that was once lost and is now found, was dead and is now alive. This is an eternal miracle. A single salvation brings great joy to all of heaven. Jesus wants to help us rescue these lost ones. "Jesus, give us your heart and passion for your lost children that we meet each day. Help us to love them back to life with your kindness and great power. Holy Spirit, anoint us to preach the gospel and to set the captives free. Jesus, bring the masses home to the Father's house!"

Disneyland Outbreak

I went down to Los Angeles to visit my friend, Jason Tax, for a week. Who knew what adventures the Holy Spirit might lead us into? On the drive down, I saw a Disneyland sign and remembered the times of lying on my bed dreaming with the Holy Spirit about revival breaking out inside the theme park. I thought, "Wow! That would be cool if that ever happened for real." In Los Angeles I had the privilege of speaking at my friend's church on Wednesday night. After the service, a lady asked me if I wanted a free ticket to Disneyland the following day. I thought, "Yea, Jesus! Those tickets are $94!"

Jason Tax, Hannah Ford[1] and I went to Disneyland to go on rides and pray for others. During lunch God set us up to meet a young man whose shoulder was in a sling. We approached him and asked if we could pray for healing. Jesus instantly touched his shoulder. He removed his sling and began to test it out. He told us that he hadn't been able to raise it at all, because of a fresh torn rotary cuff injury. He then started raising his arm over his head and moving it as freely as the other one. He started crying from God's goodness. His friends explained how he is the star football player at their school and he would have had to take the entire year off from football after his scheduled surgery. We explained the Gospel of Jesus Christ to the group of eight or so, and they all got saved and filled with the Holy Spirit. One of them got healed of scoliosis and another guy's leg grew out as their friends looked on. These teenagers got really excited.

Heavenly momentum hit and an all-out Holy Spirit healing service erupted in the Disneyland food court. It went on for four and a half hours as groups of young people came back with their friends for healing. They would come to us and say, "Can you heal this?" as they would point to a lump on their friend's knee or a bad ankle. We would answer something like, "We cannot heal anything, but Jesus can heal everything, and that same Jesus is in you now, so everyone put your hand on this person and say, 'Be healed, in Jesus' name! Now test it out.' Really, that's how we prayed, "Be healed! Now test it out." Almost every healing was instant as the looks of shock appeared on their faces. Then, praise and cheers to Jesus would erupt from the crowd of youth!

Flat feet were healed as arches formed in front of our eyes. One girl was so scared as her friends dragged her up to us. We told her, "Hun, you have nothing to be afraid of. This is Jesus, and He loves you very much." She had extreme scoliosis and a dislocated thumb that was in a hand brace. She was still very much afraid, so we told her, "We won't even need to touch you because the glory is here. Just remove your brace and move your thumb around." She did and her thumb was instantly healed. We asked her to touch her toes and then check her back out. She did and her friends lifted up the back of her shirt to check out her spine. They all screamed, because it was now perfectly straight. Jesus! We asked her if she knew Jesus, and she said, "No." We told her it was Jesus who had just healed her and asked her if she would like to know that Jesus. She said, "Yes!" We prayed with her to receive Jesus and then we explained to her about being filled with the Holy Spirit. She said she wanted Him, too!

We witnessed bone knots dissolve from knees, asthma healed, crooked knees straighten out, and eyes healed. Two boys that had protruding rib cages were pulled back to normal in their chest. Even gold dust showed up on some of them. My favorite thing was seeing these kids get saved and touched by the Holy Spirit. Almost everyone felt a strong manifestation of the Holy Spirit like electricity, heat, tingling on their bodies or a heavy, weighty presence.

The teenagers would ask us questions like, "Can you make the sadness I feel inside of me leave?" All their friends would say, "I feel that way, too." We started praying in large groups, commanding depression to leave them and joy to come. Kids were crying, laughing, yelling out Jesus' name, and saying things like, "I can't believe this! This is way better than any ride here!" These kids were getting set free!

We prayed for healing for the first few kids only. Then we taught the youth that the same Spirit dwells in each of them, and we watched Jesus heal through their hands. We witnessed over one hundred miracles, most of them instant, and about eighty decisions for Christ, of which half were first-time decisions. One young man came up to me and said, "I never knew that Jesus died for me." He threw his arms in the air and yelled at the top of his lungs, "Jesus!"

FURTHER IMPACT THROUGH YOUTUBE

Hannah Ford video recorded most of that Holy Spirit breakout in Disneyland, and made a YouTube video of it. When I first saw it, I was really impressed. It was amazing! What happened next blew my mind. God had the bright idea to send that video all over the world. Over fifty nations watched it. The most amazing things started to happen. God used it to spark hunger and faith into so many hearts all over the world. People watched this video and instantly started doing what they saw. I heard about a youth group that had never prayed for the sick before. They watched the video during their normal youth service time and then started praying for each other for physical healing. Miracles started popping. They said, "We can't just stay in here. We have to do something about this!" These kids left the youth building, went out to the streets and found people that needed healing. God showed up and miracles broke loose.

Others I heard went to the emergency room and Jesus the Healer accompanied them. I heard of many miracles from that emergency room visit. These youth had never been to supernatural ministry school. They had never been to a signs and wonders conference, and they hadn't even read a book on how to heal the sick. They watched a 10-minute video of seeing miracles in action, and they had a crazy thought that maybe it could be possible through them too! I am telling you, it is so much easier than we think. God is just waiting to do something through us! We just can't stay indoors any longer! We have to go out there and find people that need what we have. His name is Jesus. We have Him and they need Him.

So I'm begging you, PLEASE let's go give Jesus to the world!

ENDNOTES

1.   Hannah Ford's music and resources are available at http://
     www.hannahford.com/

 **ACTION STEP**

- Watch Video # 10 – Disneyland Miracle Video

Chapter 11

SUPERNATURAL TREASURE HUNTING

"God's treasures are everywhere. They are in stores, businesses, neighborhoods, parks, schools, and even in the church. They are everywhere we go." – Kevin Dedmon

You made it. I have been waiting for this moment to introduce you to Treasure Hunting. Treasure Hunting is one of the biggest means God used to help me break into my supernatural destiny. Treasure Hunting was the outreach I was skipping out on in first year BSSM. I shared about this in Chapter One. Ironically, it is the outreach activation that I currently help oversee at BSSM.

Let me give you a quick snapshot of what Treasure Hunting is all about. You ask the Holy Spirit for supernatural clues like a location, a person's appearance, their name and specific prayer needs. You write these clues on a treasure map. Then you go out following the clues on your map, which lead you to a specific person, God's treasure! Sound fun? Well, it is.

The first recorded supernatural Treasure Hunt is found in Acts Chapter 9.

> *"So the Lord said to him, "Arise and go to the street called Straight, and inquire at the house of Judas for one called Saul of Tarsus, for behold, he is praying. And in a vision he has seen a man named Ananias coming in and putting his hand on him, so that he might receive his sight."* (Acts 9:11,12)

The Lord gave Ananias a specific location- <u>Straight street</u>, A persons name- <u>Saul</u>, and a specific prayer need- <u>blindness</u>. Ananias took these clues and went out on a supernatural mission to find and bless Saul.

> *"And Ananias went his way and entered the house; and laying his hands on him he said, "Brother Saul, the Lord Jesus, who appeared to you on the road as you came, has sent me that you may receive your sight and be filled with the Holy Spirit." Immediately there fell from his eyes something like scales, and he received his sight at once; and he arose and was baptized.* (Acts 9:17,18)

I thank God that Ananias decided to GO on this Treasure Hunt and in doing so; Paul's life and letters became one of the greatest strengths and inspirations to our Christian faith.

But before we pick up the anchor and cast off to launch this ship towards the deeper waters, I want to tell you about the father of supernatural treasure hunts. This man's life has had some of the greatest personal impact and influence in my own life. He is a hero of mine. He has been a spiritual mentor, a father figure and a good friend to me. Let me introduce to you revivalist Kevin Dedmon[1]:

Kevin Dedmon is currently a pastor at Bethel Church in Redding, California. He came to BSSM in 2002 as a first year ministry student. Kevin had already been in full-time ministry as a senior pastor of a church when he became hungry to see a revival lifestyle happen in his own life. He stepped out of full time ministry and humbled himself to become a full time student. In first year BSSM, Kevin started learning how to get words of knowledge for people's healing. One day, he thought he should write some words of knowledge on a piece of paper and then go to the mall and find the people who matched his words of knowledge and heal them.

Kevin did just that and set off on a short-term mission trip to the mall to find every clue on his paper. Little did Kevin know that this was the first of many Treasure Hunts, and God was going to launch this model of supernatural evangelism across the entire planet. Since then, supernatural Treasure Hunts have become a world wide epidemic. Kevin recently told me about an African missionary that stumbled across a tribe in a remote isolated village. This missionary was approached by a tribesman carrying Kevin's book *The Ultimate Treasure Hunt*[2]. This tribesman was holding Kevin's book! I just heard a testimony of a girl that had her treasure map lead her to a local gas station. She started ministering to the guy standing in front of the checkout counter. What she did not know was this man, the treasure, was smack dab in the middle of robbing that store. He was robbing the store at gunpoint when she walked in. She did not see the gun and unknowingly she prayed and prophesied God's plan into this man's life. He was cut to the heart, and he called to his crew in the back of the store by the safe, "Guys, we are done with this lifestyle!" They stopped in the middle of the armed robbery and they left the store, all because God saw this robber as His ultimate treasure.

I truly believe Treasure Hunts have been monumental in helping to get the Church out of the church in our generation. It has helped believers that feel the least evangelistic to reach out to others with the Gospel in marketplace settings. I believe Treasure Hunts have changed the course of evangelism in our generation and time will only tell of its ultimate impact.

Treasure Hunting is unique because it isn't necessarily designed for those that have the gift of evangelism. It isn't limited only to the bold, fearless personality. Even the shyest, most timid person can set off into their supernatural destiny using a Treasure Hunt. My life is a great example of this. Treasure Hunting is not only fun, but it is for all ages, people groups and personality types. Many lives have been changed powerfully with the love of Jesus through Treasure Hunts. Many of the miracle testimonies in this book were stories from Treasure Hunting.

I am going to give you an introduction to Treasure Hunting, but you really should get Kevin's book *The Ultimate Treasure Hunt* for the full experience. In his book, Kevin goes in much more detail about Treasure Hunting. He shares practical how-tos of the hunt and stories of remarkable miracles along the ride. Just like the importance of having the owner's manual for your car, Kevin's book *The Ultimate Treasure Hunt* is the owner's manual for Treasure Hunts. If you want to start treasure hunting in your area, this book is a great resource for you. I am warning you now though. You just might get completely hooked on Treasure Hunts and you may never be the same again.

Most of the supernatural training we have practiced so far will be utilized in Treasure Hunting. Prophecy, words of knowledge, the basics for ministering to others will all be used. Some specific things we need to cover are: Filling out the treasure map and the approach to using the map. I will present Treasure Hunting to you as if you were going out as a group, but one person with the Holy Spirit is a great team size also. When you get bit with the Treasure Hunt bug and want to train others to go with you, you'll be prepared for group dynamics.

TREASURE MAP

Location

_____   _____   _____   _____   _____

A person's name

_____   _____   _____   _____   _____

A person's appearance

_____   _____   _____   _____   _____

What they might need prayer for

_____   _____   _____   _____   _____

The unusual

_____   _____   _____   _____   _____

Number   Taste   Sound   Smell

_____   _____   _____   _____

Filling Out the Map

There are five main categories with five blank lines to fill out per category. The categories are:

Location: These will be geographic places that will give your team clues about where to go. It may be a certain store or a park. You may get geographic markers such as a bench or a stop sign. This is a physical place where the treasures will be found.

Names: These are names of people that you will meet or names that will mean something to the people that you meet. These could be first or last names or nick names.

Appearance: These are clues that will make the treasure stand out. They can be articles of clothing and their color. An example would be red shirt. It could be other traits like tall or short hair. These appearance clues help you locate your treasure once you get to the location.

Prayer Needs: These are specific prayer needs for the treasure that you meet. Write down at least three for physical healing needs such as asthma or back pain.

Unusual: These are random clues that do not fit in the above categories. For example, black dog or yellow star. These clues are fun to find, especially if you don't see your appearance clues right away. Treasures are not always lying on the surface of the ground. You may need to dig and search to find them. That is part of the fun.

221

As an example, we had goldfish as a clue when we were in Safeway and we found our treasure by the Goldfish brand of crackers.

TASTE – SMELL – NUMBER - SOUND: Write down one taste, smell, number and sound. These are some fun clues.

One time in Raley's grocery store we were praying for our treasure in the produce aisle. The store had thunder crashing music playing over their vegetable produce. Our clue for sound happened to be <u>thunder</u>.

MY DAUGHTER CAMBREA'S TREASURE HUNT

This is a testimony from my daughter, Cambrea, who was 17 years old at the time. She found some random clues on her Treasure Hunt. Finding your clues is much of the adventure.

"I was partnered with an old guy named Bob. He was skeptical, very skeptical of the treasure hunt. We went to Safeway because Wyatt and I both had Safeway as the matching location. Bob and I went through Safeway looking for people in blue shirts with weird colored jeans. We didn't find anybody with that. Then I saw zit creme on my Treasure Hunt map and realized they have zit creme in Safeway. So we went down the aisle that had zit creme and there was a lady there in pajamas. I also had pajamas as my unusual clue. It was probably around 100 degrees in Redding at that time and it was 1 o'clock in the afternoon, so it was really weird finding someone in Safeway wearing long pajamas by the zit creme when it was 100 degrees outside. I went up and talked to her and she wanted prayer to get

---

good test scores for college. So Bob and I prayed for her about that. I didn't think I would find someone wearing pajamas at that time of the day, but I did."

FILLING OUT THE MAP

On the first couple of Treasure Hunts, I encourage you to take around five minutes to fill the entire map out leaving no blanks. Ask the Holy Spirit to give you clues, then write down the very first thoughts that you have. It will most likely feel like you are totally making these clues up, but just write them down anyway. Do not over-think trying to get the clues. Quickly write down the first clues that come to mind no matter how odd they seem. After your map is full, circle the clues that you feel more strongly about. Then see what clues you found after the Treasure Hunt. You may see that you found more of the circled clues. We are continuing to train ourselves in recognizing God's voice.

As you continue to Treasure Hunt, try new ways to get your clues. Try this method and see what happens: Take thirty minutes to soak and ask God to show you mental visions of who you will meet today. Pay attention to the screen of your mind. If you see a picture of a friend from high school, chances are you will meet someone that day with that same name. When you are trying to get clues for prayer needs, ask the Holy Spirit for physical impressions and be aware of God's presence resting on a certain part of your body. You can also ask the Holy Spirit to show you a mental image of a body part and write that down. Ask to hear the still, small voice and listen to what you hear in your heart. Write down what you hear. This is a great way to activate your spiritual senses.

Your senses will become sharper with practice.

Get Into Teams and GO

We normally get in teams of four or five people, a normal car-load. Try to have equal numbers of girls and guys on each team. This will help your team approach people of any gender. Once you are in your group, look at all your location clues as a team. Decide as a group which location seems to stand out the most and as a team go to that location. Read all of your clues to each other and use each other's clues, because this is a team effort. One person may have the location Wal-Mart and another may have blue shirt, another left knee. The Holy Spirit will use all our maps as a team. He knows how to bring unity that way.

Looking for Clues and the Introduction

Once at your location, start looking for other clues from the maps. To give you an example, I am going to use the clues from above: Wal-Mart, blue shirt and left knee. You are walking around Wal-Mart and you spot a man with a blue shirt and he is wearing a black brace on his left knee. Have no more than two people approach him, hopefully with a guy. An introduction would be something like this: "Hi, this might sound odd but we are on a Treasure Hunt and we think we found our treasure, you." Show him all the clues on the map that led you to him. As you point out the clues, you can say, "See, we have Wal-Mart, blue shirt and left knee. Introduce your team and show him all the clues on your treasure map. Ask him if any of the other clues make sense to him. Somewhere in the conversation bring it back to the left knee. "By the way what happened to your left knee?" Ask the pain scale and mobility and release healing. Practice getting prophetic words too. Your whole aim is to bless this person's socks off with the kingdom of God. Keep going and growing, and give yourself grace to learn.

PROPHETIC ART

Prophetic art is inspired art from God. I was not a big fan of using prophetic art for supernatural ministry when I was first asked to do it. I actually had a pretty negative attitude toward it. I thought, "That picture looks so childish...no talent there...leave the kindergarten refrigerator art at home. I want to heal the sick, cast out devils and raise the dead, not draw with crayons!" My outlook toward prophetic pictures in marketplace ministry has changed 180 degrees now. I have seen God do the most remarkable out-of-the-box miracles through childish looking pictures drawn by all age groups with colored pencils or crayons.

Before we go out on Treasure Hunts, we typically take blank computer paper and colored pencils and draw whatever comes to mind. We usually take about five minutes to do this. Some make prophetic cards and others a simple picture. You can write a message to go with it. Some people have drawn pictures of body parts that needed healing with a slash running through it representing "no more pain". People have been healed by just holding onto those pictures without prayer. They felt the pain leave their bodies as they touched the paper. If God can use handkerchiefs to heal the sick, He can certainly use paper also. God is so creative that he uses the simple things to confound the wise. On the Treasure Hunt, we give the cards away to the treasure we find or other people that the Holy Spirit highlights. It is loads of fun!

First Time Treasure Hunts

I was helping with a supernatural lifestyle conference a couple years ago. Most of the attendees were middle-aged folks from conservative church backgrounds. Most of them had never prayed for the sick in the church, let alone in the marketplace. They had been trained for a day on healing, getting words of knowledge and basic prophecy. It was our job to train them in Treasure Hunts and to send them out into the community to minister supernaturally. We also had them do prophetic art. This conference took place during the summer, so most of the BSSM students who were more experienced treasure hunters were gone. This not-so-confident group of fearless leaders had to show them the ropes. We helped them form teams and then we sent them out saying, "See you in a couple hours. You got this!" They looked like a bunch of sheep that were just sent out to the slaughterhouse. I heard some of them saying amongst themselves, "The flyer said Treasure Hunt training. I thought they were just going to teach us how to do a Treasure Hunt. I didn't realize they were actually going to send us out to do one." To be honest I was feeling rather nervous for them too.

Two hours later, an entirely different group of people entered the building. I hardly recognized them. This was not the timid crowd that we forced out into the world a couple of hours ago. Something had happened to them. This bunch had come alive! I thought to myself, "Who are these giddy excited people?" They started coming up and telling us what God had just done through them. It was not even the official testimonial time, yet a lady exclaimed, "Oh my gosh! You won't believe what just happened..." Then another lady almost interrupting the last one, "I have to tell you what God just did through us!" This entire team surrounded us looking like a bunch of wide-eyed teenagers, all nodding their heads in unison with each detail of the story. What had happened to this group? This well-mannered timid bunch had morphed into a group of enthused Crazy Jesus people!

"After this the Lord appointed seventy-two others and sent them two by two ahead of him to every town and place where he was about to go...Heal the sick who are there and tell them, 'The kingdom of God has come near to you'...The seventy-two returned with great joy!" (Luke 10 NIV). Like the seventy-two that Jesus sent out; these people had a taste of a supernatural lifestyle and destiny that had been waiting for them. Something was unlocked inside of them now and they had great joy seeing that the kingdom of God could flow through them.

Next a group of three very happy ladies in their early 50s came up to share, "You know how you made us draw those silly pictures? These two ladies and I ended up on the same team. We were not sitting together and we all drew the same picture. We all drew a yellow flower with purple around the edges. Then we went to Wal-Mart and I had the number 13 as a clue. We decided to start by going to aisle 13 to look for our treasure. We almost fell over in shock with what we saw. A lady was walking down aisle 13 heading straight towards us carrying these flowers. (They held up a bouquet of four plastic flowers that were yellow with purple around the edges.) We brought these back to show you. Don't they look exactly like the ones we drew?" They held up one of the drawings of the yellow flower with purple edges that they drew. I couldn't believe it myself. I thought, 'This is nuts, God!' (The photo of the flowers and the picture is in this chapter video.) They continued, "But you have got to hear the rest. That young lady had bought those flowers because her mother had died a year ago and those flowers were for her grave. When we showed that precious girl our pictures and told her why we had drawn them, she started weeping right there in our arms. I'm telling you, this is God! We got to even show her another clue on our map, loss in the family. We got to really love on this young lady and let her know that God sees her and He loves her and He is going to help her in her pain. This was one of the most powerful things that I got to be a part of. By the way, when are we doing our next Treasure Hunt? Can we do one over dinner break?"

The next testimony is from a tall stocky muscular man in his mid-40s. Grinning with the enthusiasm of a teenager, he tells his story, "Okay, you won't believe this. You know how we filled out those maps. When I got to the clue for smell, I actually started to smell bleach in my nose. It was as if my wife was doing laundry. I was shocked. I also drew a picture of a heavier set girl with a blue dress with thin straps that hold it up. I had never done anything like this before and was very skeptical. Our team goes to Safeway and the second we step foot inside the building, I start smelling that bleach again. It was very strong, so I told the team we should go find the laundry bleach. When we found the bleach, I couldn't believe my eyes. The heavy set lady in the blue dress precisely like I drew was standing right next to the bleach! Okay, I have to be honest, I got real scared. I didn't know what to do, so I covered up my picture that I drew of the lady. I did not want my team to see it. I looked around like we were still trying to find our clues. My heart was pounding and finally that lady walked off. I was so overcome by it all! After a few moments I couldn't take it any longer. I showed the team my picture and they said, "That's the lady that was standing right here!" So they dragged me along and we found that lady a few aisles over and explained the whole Treasure Hunt thing. We showed her the picture I had drawn of her. She couldn't believe this was happening. We showed her our maps and found out her right ankle and lower back was in pain, and we had those clues also on our map. We prayed for her ankle and it was fifty percent better right away. We prayed again and all the pain was gone. Her back was healed one hundred percent, as well. All this happened in a grocery store! I am amazed! I was really scared, but after we stepped out I couldn't believe how easy and fun this was!"

I could write an entire chapter from testimonies just from that one conference. These folks came alive stepping out in love and seeing God touch lives through them. So will you!

Ask some friends to go on a Treasure Hunt with you or go by yourself. Do a Treasure Hunt this week. Draw a prophetic art piece to give away. Finding clues on your map is great, but getting to see someone's eyes light up with hope after they experience the reality of God's love for them is priceless. Go find God's treasure and release His good mood and kingdom on them. Try to make Treasure Hunting a regular steady part of your supernatural lifestyle.

ENDNOTES

1. Kevin Dedmon's resources are available at http://www.kevindedmon.com

2. *The Ultimate Treasure Hunt* is available at http://store.ibethel.org/p1156/the-ultimate-treasure-hunt

 **ACTION STEP**

- Watch Video #11 - Supernatural Treasure Hunting

Chapter 12

The New Normal

"If you get close enough you can hear a 'popping' sound as the new limb grows out." – Jim Rogers

I hope you had an amazing Treasure Hunt. I'm sure many lives were touched with God's love and they will never be the same. Way to go! Having specific times of ministry in public like Treasure Hunts help us to build more courage. We also should develop a supernatural lifestyle helping others wherever we go without a map. I encourage you to keep doing planned outreach events but also begin to practice stepping out throughout your normal day. Practice getting words of knowledge and prophetic words on the fly at restaurants, grocery stores, the bank, wherever you go.

A supernatural non-compartmentalized lifestyle is what we are pursuing. We want our entire life to be an outreach of love. Jesus healed the sick as He went during his normal day. Throughout your activities each day, be aware of any revelation that Holy Spirit is communicating with you about others around you. Take risks to step out and bless them. You can brighten one person's life today with the power and love of Jesus. Todd White often gives fishing lead sinker weights out to the class during his evangelism schools. He says, "Put this in your pocket and when you do not feel led to reach out to love on someone, reach into your pocket and feel this. Now you feel lead to minister to them." He also states, "Every day you walk by someone because you do not feel led to stop for them. Show me how Jesus has not died for that person also." Todd's point is that everyone is waiting for a God encounter through you. *"Go into all the world and preach the Good news to everyone"* (Mark 16:15 NLT). No place and no one is excluded. Jesus has paid the entire price for every person and every need they have. Let's do this thing in Jesus' name! Let's have a normal Jesus life, loving and setting people free everywhere we go.

NEW LIMBS GROW BACK

During April of 2011, I was invited to a Bethel Church healing room training to hear my friends, Josh and Kris, speak. It was then I heard a testimony that would forever alter my life. An email testimony was read about Jim Rogers[1] who is an associate pastor of Bridge Way Church in Denver, Colorado. Jim has been traveling the world for many years preaching the Gospel of Jesus with miraculous signs following him. The email was about miracles that Jim had witnessed while doing a South African crusade. He had witnessed other-worldly signs, wonders and miracles. A pillar of smoke and a glory cloud appeared. Jim got to witness many, I repeat, many complete new arms and legs grow back right in front of his eyes.

Okay, stop and re-read that last sentence as many times as you need to. These people had no limbs and within a few seconds God recreated complete new arms and legs. We are talking only a shoulder and NO arm and--voila--a complete brand NEW arm! Did you hear that? Complete brand new limbs grew back! Jim said they didn't even have hair on them. It took a few minutes for the hair to grow. They were fresh out of the box. Along with those miracles, two people were raised from the dead and around 150,000 were saved!

Needless to say, everyone that heard the testimony was utterly awestruck. This email was read over and over at the Bethel staff meeting that morning, pulling on the power of this testimony. We now had a new mark in the sand! No longer was it a testimony of a glory cloud appearing and limbs growing out at Azusa Street a hundred years ago. This testimony wasn't even a day old. It was fresh. We all realized the same Spirit that pulled those limbs out of boxes in heaven and put them on those bodies, He lives in us, too!

Follow me on a short rabbit trail for a minute. It goes somewhere really good, I promise. Last summer, I took my two boys to their first professional baseball game. I was about to click the key on my computer to buy tickets for the Oakland A's when a friend walked into the dining room saying, "What are you doing?" My friend convinced me that we should go watch the San Francisco Giants instead, since they had won the World Series the year before. The prices of the tickets were similar, so I decided to watch the

Giants play. Denver, Colorado happened to be the opposing team. We drove down to San Francisco and had an all-out amazing day, watching professional baseball and eating foot-long German franks, overlooking the gorgeous San Francisco Bay. It was wonderful. By the way, if you are wondering, the San Francisco Giants lost to the Denver Colorado Rockies, two to one.

Several weeks later, I was in my room and the Holy Spirit spoke to my heart, "Jason, the baseball game that you went to was prophetic, and you don't even realize it." I said, "Huh?...What?... Say that again?"

He said, "Jason, the baseball game that you and your boys went to was prophetic."

I replied in my heart, "Okay, go on...?"

Holy Spirit: "So what happened at the game?"

Me: "The Giants lost to Denver, Colorado, two to one...and?"

Holy Spirit: "Jason, Who do you know from Denver, Colorado?"

Me: "Um...I don't think that I know anyone from Denver, Colorado...

After a moment I thought, "Hmm...Was that guy with the crazy limbs testimony from Denver?"

I looked up that email testimony, and, sure enough, Jim Rogers was from Denver, Colorado.

So I replied "Yeah, that guy Jim Rogers, he is from Denver, Colorado."

Then the Holy Spirit dropped this heavily on me, "Jason, the creative miracles that I released on Jim Rogers' life are going to destroy giants in the land. These giants are mindsets of what my people think is possible. These lids of limitation are the giants that are going to be defeated. Creative limb restoration is going to start happening all over the world, not just in Africa, but also in every nation by every kind of person. What is considered to be unusual miracles now will be normal in the near future. There is going to soon be a new normal. Everything is about to change! Jason, to prove this to you, the date that you and your boys went to the baseball game is a verse in the Bible about giants."

Excited I respond, "Yes, Holy Spirit, this is awesome! Okay, I am going to see if this is really you now." I fumbled around my room, speaking to myself, "When did I go to the game?" I couldn't remember, so I looked up my electronic baseball tickets. The date of the game was on June the fourth or 6/4. I knew it would be represented as 6:4 since I was looking for a Bible verse. I grabbed my Bible and flipped to Genesis 6:4. My jaw hit the floor...

> *"There were giants in the earth in those days; and also after that, when the sons of God came in unto the daughters of men, and they bear children to them, the same became mighty men which were of old, men of renown"* (Genesis 6:4).

I was completely beside myself, "Father, what am I supposed to do about this?" The Lord said, "I want you to honor what is on Jim Rogers' life." In time I was able to make contact with Jim through a friend, and now I have had the great privilege of developing a friendship with him. Jim is truly an anointed and humble man of

God. I have been very blessed and inspired by his life.

The Great Convergence

The testimony from Jim Rogers and the prophetic word the Lord gave me are what I believe we, the Body of Christ, are about to step into. It is a realm of the supernatural that has never been demonstrated on such a worldwide scale. There is going to be a new normal of God's power and love exploits. What could that possibly look like? I believe God has given us some insight and glimpses into what is coming by some of God's great Generals. Could we be on the convergence of one, if not the greatest, awakening in history? Could this epic move of God happen in our generation?

On the same day in 1909, William Seymour and Charles Parham, hundreds of miles apart, both prophesied that God's Shekinah glory (the visible glory of God) would return to earth after 100 years.[2] This time it would not be in just one location as during the Azusa street revival in Los Angeles. It would be everywhere.

Smith Wigglesworth prophesied, "I see the greatest revival in the history of mankind coming to planet Earth, maybe as never before. I see every form of disease healed. I see whole hospitals emptied with no one there. Even the doctors are running down the streets shouting. There would be untold numbers of uncountable multitudes that would be saved. No man will say so many, so many, because nobody will be able to count those who come to Jesus. No disease will be able to stand before God's people...It will be a worldwide situation, not local, a worldwide thrust of God's power and God's anointing upon mankind."[3]

William Branham said, "God is going to take every move of God in history, and even what we witnessed and what we saw in Bible days, and put it all together in one great Holy Ghost bomb and drop it on Planet Earth and the nations will rock and reel with the power of God like we've never seen. Prime Time News, not the late night talk shows and not the preachers, the Prime Time News will show the dead being raised and limbs created and eyes being put back in eye sockets and arms stretching out. Preachers won't lay their hands on them like we did; they will simply speak the word and blindness will leave. There'll be so many people, no auditorium, no church and no arena will hold the people. And no tent. They'll even stand in an open field. It's going to happen in America."[4]

PARTNERING WITH GOD

I want to share what I believe God is saying about the part we play in this upcoming move of God. I believe God has told me that body parts growing back is a heavenly invitation being released into the earth. However, it is going to take sons and daughters of God to birth this thing into existence. God is making it available to us, but we need to partner with Him, stepping out in faith to bring it forth.

Years ago in Toronto, Canada, Randy Clark prophesied over missionary Heidi Baker. She was told, "The blind will see, the cripple will walk, the dead will be raised and the poor will hear the Good News of Jesus Christ." She excitedly went back to Mozambique with the word of the Lord and started laying hands on the blind. The only problem was the blind were not seeing. In fact, Heidi prayed for two hundred blind people for about a year before the very first person was healed. Heidi has continued to pray for the blind and now around seventy percent of the blind she prays for are healed. Her ministry has seen over one hundred people raised from the dead. Deafness is healed one hundred percent of the time when the Gospel is preached for the first time in a new village in Africa.

The prophetic invitation from the Lord was released over Heidi's life the second Randy Clark declared it. Heidi had to trust the Lord's word and embrace the invitation that God had for her life. God gave Heidi the invitation, but Heidi needed to birth that invitation into a reality by being consistent and praying for the blind until eyes started to open.

I am strongly assured that the Lord is extending to us a great invitation into unequaled possibilities right now. It is an invitation to step into things that have never been seen on a broad global scale. Heaven is overflowing with new limbs and God is asking us to trust him and pray, believing that limbs will grow back. We may pray for many or just one before we see it happen. I feel God is asking us, "Will you trust Me, pray and birth this into the world?" Will we stop for the one, love them and pray for their missing limb to grow back? God, in His sovereignty, will not do this without us. He is waiting for us to partner with Him. God wants there to be a new normal for us to walk in. He wants this new creative limb mindset of possibility and expectancy to be released for His glory. It will require us to partner with Him.

Jim Rogers' Testimony

As you read this testimony, remember that it is a testimony of Jesus, which is the spirit of prophecy. God wants to do it again through you and me. Let this testimony sink deep within your heart, and ask the Holy Spirit how you can help birth this into our generation.

Jim Rogers left for a South Africa ministry trip in April 2011. They experienced nightly crowds of over 100,000 people. During the afternoon pastors' meeting, a pastor came up to Jim and said, "Jim, come look. There is a glory cloud!" Jim went over and saw a pillar of cloud around five or six feet in diameter. It was so thick you couldn't see through it. He said there was gold dust and feathers swirling on the outside perimeter of the pillar. A memory of Randy Clark having people walk through a similar glory cloud came into Jim's thoughts, so he had people that needed healing walk through the cloud. He reported they were instantly healed walking through that cloud, throwing down their crutches and canes on the other side. I asked Jim if he had walked through the cloud, and, if so, what the experience was like. Jim's response: "Of course, I walked through it. I felt the biggest hug from Father God. I didn't want to leave. I wanted to stay right there in it."

In the nightly outdoor crusade the cloud showed up again! This time it was in the form of a large cloud resting on different sections of the crowd. As the cloud rested on these sections, people were healed of every kind of disease. The deaf could hear, the blind could see, the crippled were restored in the cloud of God's presence. Jim said there was a group of lepers, about forty-five in number. They were quarantined with a several foot perimeter around them in case they had wet contagious leprosy. I imagine this group looked horrific, almost zomby-ish. Jim stated their skin was oozing pus and many were missing ears, noses, fingers, toes, hair and skin. The leprosy demon had literally been eating them alive for years, one body part at a time. But God looked at the group with great compassion. The cloud came right down and rested on that leprous bunch for about ten to fifteen minutes, completely engulfing them. Jim said when it lifted, there were no longer any lepers; only normal people like you and me. They had new ears, noses, fingers and toes, as well as new hair and skin. Jesus had recreated these missing body parts and had given these people their lives back!

When the crowd saw this, they started to jump over chairs, mobbing their brothers and sisters with lots of physical embraces and tears. Many of these lepers had not felt a single human touch for several years. Jim said it was such a powerful and profound emotional moment. The great multitude of Africans erupted in exuberant thanksgiving, praise and worship to our crowned King!

During the daily pastor's meeting, a local pastor was missing his right hand. It had been cut off during the war. Jim felt the Holy Spirit say to pray for his hand to grow back. As this pastor was worshiping, Jim prayed for God to give this man his hand back. In that moment, the black leather cap that covered the pastor's stump popped off as a new mass of flesh and fingers shot out. A brand new hand was created in Jesus' name! How incredible! Your mind might be having problems keeping up with these events. That's okay. Jim said even being there and witnessing these events with his own eyes was completely mind-boggling. He said his brain would interrogate what his eyes had just witnessed. Completely awestruck, Jim would ask himself, "Did I really just see that?" At times Jim said the pastors and he sat on the stage and watched in wonder at what God was doing. It was like having front row tickets to one of the most incredible events in history. At one point there was a stack of crutches and canes fifteen feet high on the stage from people that were healed. The walking sticks were no longer needed.

At the nightly crusade, Jim asked anybody that was missing body parts to come to the front. About 150 people came forward. Most were missing legs, and about ten to twelve people were missing arms. Jim reported that many had lost their legs because of land mine accidents. As they prayed for new limbs to grow out, Jim looked in childlike amazement as many new limbs shot out to full length within a few seconds. He said, "It doesn't take long to grow a new arm or leg, just a couple seconds." When I asked Jim what it looks like when they come out, he said, "The first thing that happens is the skin that covers the stump has to be popped, so if you get close enough you actually hear a 'popping' sound. Then a full-sized limb starts to shoot out at a very fast pace. If it is a leg, when it gets to the heel the growth changes direction to make the foot. Then the toes come out at the last. It happens really fast, so you really have to be watching." He said that it looks like how a computer program would animate a leg growing out of nowhere. Jim also noted that the limbs are hairless and look clean-shaven when they grow out. The hair begins to grow back in a few minutes.

Okay, take a deep breath. There is more. The last morning at the pastor's house, there was a knock at the door. This pastor's house was situated in a secluded remote location. Jim said when the pastor opened the door, there was a strong odorous stench of death. At the door was a man with a dead girl's body in his arms. It was a father holding his lifeless eight-year-old daughter. The man said that four days ago his daughter had died. As he was crying out, God gave him this exact address. He had written down this pastor's address on a piece of paper that God had spoken to him supernaturally. This father had been carrying his dead daughter in his arms for the last four days from an outlying village in search of this pastor's house.

Jim said the body was already decomposing because of the high temperature and humidity. This girl's skin was rotting and she smelled terrible. The pastor and companions decided to put the girl's dead body on a large coffee table in the living room, and they started praying for her in tongues. There were about twenty-five people praying in the group. Jim said, "The presence of God came in so thick, it was almost unreal. We had a hard time just standing as we prayed for her. All of a sudden her eyelids fluttered and she sat up. From the time she lay flat on the table until she sat up, her skin was made perfectly and completely normal." This young girl was given back to her father, raised from the dead by the power and love of God!

One of the pastor's assistants took the father and the raised-from-the-dead daughter back to their village. About thirty minutes later there was another knock at the door. This time there were two men holding a makeshift stretcher carrying a dead boy's body. The dead boy was fifteen years old. This boy's father was also given the pastor's address supernaturally from God. The father and his friend went to the morgue and picked the son up off the cold stone slab. He had been shot in the chest and had been dead for three days. They put the boy who was only wearing boxers on the large coffee table and started to pray. Jim said, "The boy's body started to vibrate, and then his body started to bounce up and down on the coffee table. His body started to bounce so hard that I thought the coffee table might break. This happened for a while. Then all of a sudden he woke up. His dad had brought a pair of pants and a shirt for him to wear, demonstrating the father's faith that God was going to do something."

I don't know about you, but these accounts really get me stirred up! I can no longer act like the solution to every impossible situation isn't living inside of me! Jesus in us is just waiting to get out to help others. We cannot just read a testimony like this and think, "This is a nice story about Jim Rogers." No! We must embrace the fact that this story of outlandish miracles is about the same God that is inside of US! It's important we personalize this testimony, realizing the Spirit that did all these miracles is the same Spirit who is with us. The very same Holy Spirit lives in you and me!

> *"The Spirit of God, who raised Jesus from the dead, lives in you. And just as God raised Christ Jesus from the dead, he will give life to your mortal bodies by this same Spirit living within you"* (Romans 8:11 NLT).

At first Jim was not convinced that he was supposed to do this crusade because of the volatile climate of the area. Others had actually suggested that he not go at this time because of the impending danger. Jim inquired of the Lord and he heard the Holy Spirit say, "Go." He trusted God and went. In doing so, Jim had the extraordinary privilege of witnessing one of the greatest demonstrations of God's healing power and His manifest presence recorded in modern day history.

I believe God is asking us this same question. Will we go, too? It may not be to the same places that others have gone, but will we do something with this powerful Gospel of Jesus? What are we saving ourselves for? Do we want to leave a big mark on this earth in our lifetime or our we going to go out with a whimper...the choice is ours. What are we going to do?

LOVE SAYS GO

Most likely we will never feel completely ready, qualified, competent or anointed enough to accomplish what God is asking us to do. I like what Graham Cooke says, "God is asking us to do the impossible. So we will never feel comfortable in what He is asking us to do. We can only get our comfort in Who God is."

As we spend time in His presence and abide in His great love, love itself will possess us. The love of God will cause us to get out of our personal winepress of fear and do great exploits with Him. The love of God will compel us to reach out to give God an opportunity to invade the impossible situations that surround us.

If our motivation is love, whether the limb grows back or not, we cannot fail because that is what the scale of heaven measures... Love. If we stop for the one and we did not see the miracle that we had hoped for, we still did our part. We trusted in a good supernatural God and we had the great honor to stop and love someone today. If we can make someone's life a little brighter because of the light and love of God working through us--that is ministry. We get to plant almighty seeds of the kingdom of God inside of the people we encounter every day. We must trust that God is the good harvester. Sometimes we plant seeds or water them but God brings the harvest.

With all that said, don't be entirely surprised when you stop to pray for the deaf and the deaf ears begin to pop open. Or when the blind eyes start seeing because that is God's good nature. When you pray for those needing a new limb, listen intently for that popping noise and do not blink. Remember, these limbs can shoot out so fast that you almost miss seeing it. Just make sure you let the person with that brand new hairless limb know, "Don't worry about the absence of hair. It will grow back in a minute."

God wants there to be a new normal for us to bring forth in our generation. He is ready to slay the old mindsets of normal lids of limitation. We have an historic opportunity lying in the balance to co-labor with God in this. Heaven is primed and ready to release a realm of extreme creative miracles and limb restoration. It will require us to partner with Him and pray for the impossible to bring it forth. Will we be the ones to hear His voice, believe Him and GO?

I hear a resounding, "YES!" Let's do this thing in Jesus' name! The Almighty King of Kings is with us, so who can be against us! Love never fails, and Love Says Go!

ENDNOTES

1.   Jim Rogers' resources are available at http://www.experiencin ghispresence.org/

2.   William Seymour and Charles Parham 100 year prophecy, http://healingandrevival.com/BooksWJSeymour.htm http://www.youtube.com/watch?v=UzhKIViD0RU

3.   Prophecy Given by Smith Wigglesworth - 1947 Revival Spreading from England to Europe, http://propheticanointing. tripod.com/id13.html

4.   William Branham prophecy, from Buford Dowell June 1965. http://www.whitedoveministries.org/index.cfm?zone=Docs/ April2009.htm&page=Articles

 **Action Step**

- Watch Video #12 – Jim Rogers' Testimony & Imparta-tion

About Jason Chin

Jason Chin is based out of Bethel Church in Redding California. He has the great privilege to teach and train at supernatural conferences around the globe. Jason's core message is hosting God's presence and the finished work of the cross. His main passion is beholding the face of Jesus and sharing Him everywhere he goes.

NOW AVAILABLE!
JOIN OUR NEXT 12 WEEK ONLINE
SUPERNATURAL MINISTRY SCHOOL

Enroll at www.LSGacademy.org

LSGA is a 12 week online school designed to take you to the next level. With weekly teaching and activation steps you will grow. It is a community of hungry students from all around the world that are going after a supernatural lifestyle.

When you register enter this Promotion Code and save $20 off the LSGA tuition: **LSGA20**

CONTACT US AT: lovesaysgoteam@gmail.com